∞

*The Basic Book
of the Eucharist*

Other books
from Sophia Institute Press®
by the Reverend Lawrence G. Lovasik:

The Hidden Power of Kindness

The Basic Book of Catholic Prayer

The Catholic Family Handbook

The Basic Book

of the

Eucharist

by the Reverend
Lawrence G. Lovasik

SOPHIA INSTITUTE PRESS®
Manchester, New Hampshire

Sophia Institute Press
Box 5284, Manchester, NH 03108
1-800-888-9344
www.SophiaInstitute.com
Sophia Institute Press® is a registered trademark of Sophia Institute.

Imprimi potest: Raymond J. Weisenberger, S.V.D.
Provincial, Girard, Pennsylvania
Nihil obstat: Wilfrid J. Nash, Litt.D., *Censor Librorum*
Imprimatur: John Mark Gannon, D.D., D.C.L., LL.D.
Archbishop of Erie, Pennsylvania
December 8, 1959

Library of Congress Cataloging-in-Publication Data

Lovasik, Lawrence G. (Lawrence George), 1913-
    The basic book of the Eucharist / Lawrence G. Lovasik.
        p. cm.
    Abridged ed. of: The Eucharist in Catholic life.
    Includes bibliographical references.
    ISBN 1-928832-22-9 (pbk. : alk. paper)
    1. Lord's Supper — Catholic Church. 2. Mass. I. Lovasik, Lawrence G. (Lawrence George), 1913- Eucharist in Catholic life. II. Title.

BX2215.3 .L68 2001
264'.02036 — dc21   00-053832

To Jesus Christ,
the Divine Word of God Incarnate
and Eternal High Priest,
who said, "I am the Bread of Life,"
in deepest gratitude for the Sacrifice of the Mass,
Holy Communion, and His Real Presence among us,
through the hands of
Our Lady of the Most Blessed Sacrament,
this book is reverently dedicated

∞

Contents

Part Three

Holy Communion

∽

Foreword

The Holy Eucharist is the crown of all God's achievements. It is the richest, the most mysterious, the most appealing, and the tenderest of all. This sacrament of sacraments gathers into its depths the unsearchable riches of Christ. Into the Eucharist flow the goodness, the wisdom, the power, the mercy, and the generosity of God.

Devotion to the Holy Eucharist, therefore, is surely the greatest means to make you more interior, more Christlike, because the Eucharist is the source from which the graces of Redemption continually flow to mankind.

In a world radio address in 1943, Pope Pius XII said, "The thought of the Eucharist is the center of the faith now as it was in the first centuries. Its increase in the Church and its spiritual, vivifying radiation must become more vital and more effective."

These words of the Holy Father point out the purpose of this book — namely, that the spiritual influence of the Eucharist may become more vital and more effective in the lives of Catholics.

May Catholics heed the voice of Holy Mother Church and return to the Eucharist-mindedness of the first Christians. May the last will of Jesus be carried out as faithfully today as it was then. Daily Mass with Holy Communion is the Church's ideal. The altar is the center of the Christ-life — the center for the priest who there offers the eucharistic Sacrifice; the center for the faithful who gather in the churches before the altar to strengthen their souls at the Lord's Table. The Eucharist is the food of life — food of Catholic life, which therefore ought to be a eucharistic life.

I entrust these pages to the loving care of Our Lady of the Most Blessed Sacrament.

Father Lawrence G. Lovasik
Feast of Christ the King
Divine Word Seminary
Girard, Pennsylvania

∞

*The Basic Book
of the Eucharist*

Part One

∞

Christ's Real Presence
in the Eucharist

Chapter One

∽

Recognize Christ's Presence
in the Eucharist

Jesus proposed the doctrine of the Holy Eucharist to His disciples a full year before He died. The sixth chapter of St. John's Gospel is concerned primarily with Christ's preparation of His disciples for the institution of the Holy Eucharist. The promise of the Eucharist is stated clearly.

The morning after Jesus had miraculously fed the multitude, the people came to Him again. They hoped that He would repeat His miracle and again satisfy their hunger. He told them, "You seek me, not because you saw signs, but because you ate your fill of the loaves."[1]

Then He sought to lift their thoughts above earthly nourishment, by speaking to them of spiritual food for the soul. "Do not labor for the food which perishes, but for the food which endures to eternal life, which the Son of Man will give to you."[2]

The Jews then asked what they should do to obtain this spiritual food. Jesus taught them that they could obtain it by believing that He was the Messiah and Son of God, whom the Father had

---

[1] John 6:26.
[2] John 6:27.

sent and who alone could give them this food. They cried out in delight, "Lord, give us this bread always."[3] They still thought that this heavenly food was some wondrous bread, something like the manna from Heaven that fed the Israelites in the desert.

Jesus first spoke of Himself as the Bread of Life that the Father had already given the world. He was the Bread of Life that the soul receives by an act of faith. Then Jesus spoke of something in the future, something that He would give. The Bread that Jesus promised was His Flesh. Not the Father, but Jesus Himself would give it to His faithful followers. They would receive it not merely spiritually, that is, by believing in Him as the Messiah and the very Son of God made man, but really and truly, by *eating* it.

That such is the meaning of Christ's words we know also from the way in which He compares this new food with the manna from Heaven that fed the Israelites in the desert. Jesus said, "Your fathers ate the manna in the wilderness, and they died. This is the Bread which comes down from Heaven, that a man may eat of it and not die."[4]

He continued, "I am the living Bread which came down from Heaven; if any one eats of this Bread, he will live forever; and the Bread which I shall give for the life of the world is my Flesh."[5]

When the Jews argued among themselves, asking, "How can this man give us his flesh to eat?"[6] Jesus pointed out that His words are to be taken literally. "Truly, truly, I say to you, unless you eat the flesh of the Son of Man and drink His blood, you have no life in you; he who eats my Flesh and drinks my Blood has eternal life, and I will raise him up at the last day. For my Flesh is food indeed, and my Blood is drink indeed. He who eats my Flesh and drinks

[3] John 6:34.
[4] John 6:49-50.
[5] John 6:51.
[6] John 6:52.

my Blood abides in me, and I in him. As the living Father sent me, and I live because of the Father, so he who eats me will live because of me. This is the Bread which came down from Heaven, not such as the fathers ate and died; he who eats this Bread will live forever."[7]

In these words prefaced with "Truly, truly," Jesus stresses the repetition of the ideas of flesh and blood, of eating and drinking.

St. John states that many of the people declared that this doctrine was too hard to believe. "This is a hard saying; who can listen to it?"[8] He also states that "many of His disciples drew back and no longer went about with Him."[9] But Jesus did not call them back to make a correction if they had misunderstood Him. He let them go. He was ready to allow even the Apostles to depart if they refused to believe in Him and His word, for He asked them, "Do you also wish to go away?"[10] Simon Peter therefore answered, "Lord, to whom shall we go? You have the words of eternal life; and we have believed, and have come to know, that You are the Holy One of God."[11]

∞

Christ instituted the Eucharist

More than a year had passed since Jesus had promised to give us the wondrous living Bread from Heaven. He must suffer and die in order to give us life eternal. But He did not wish to depart from this world without leaving behind a remembrance of His love for us. In His great love for mankind, Jesus found a means to make us all spiritually rich and to remain with us to the end of the world.

---

[7] John 6:53-58.
[8] John 6:60.
[9] John 6:66.
[10] John 6:67.
[11] John 6:68-69.

Before the enemies of Jesus could take away His life, His love already provided for His presence on earth in a new way — by the institution of the Most Holy Sacrament of the Altar: He gave us Himself in the Holy Eucharist.

The night of our Lord's Passion had come. Jesus and the Twelve were assembled in a room in Jerusalem and were celebrating the paschal supper, for the feast of the Passover was at hand.

There is a significant reason our Lord chose the feast of the Passover for the institution of the Blessed Sacrament. The Israelites had longed to be freed from the slavery of Pharaoh and to depart from Egypt. At God's command, the father of every family was to sacrifice a lamb without blemish, and, with his family, he was to eat its flesh. Then he was to sprinkle the side posts and the door posts of his house with the blood of the lamb. All houses that had been sprinkled with the blood of the lamb were spared by the destroying angel of the Lord, but the firstborn of every family of the Egyptians was killed. In grateful memory of this event, the Israelites celebrated the paschal supper each year.[12]

The paschal lamb was a type, or example, of the true paschal lamb, Jesus Christ, who allowed Himself to be slain as a sacrificial lamb on the Cross. He thereby freed us from the slavery of Satan. By His Blood, He willed to preserve us from eternal death in Hell and to lead us into the promised land of Heaven.

Jesus and His Apostles were gathered around the table to partake of the paschal lamb. Jesus said to His Apostles, "I have earnestly desired to eat this Passover with you before I suffer."[13] Unleavened (yeastless) bread, such as the Jews were obliged to eat at the paschal supper, lay in a dish upon the table. There was also on the table a cup of wine. St. Mark describes what happened: "And as they were eating, He took bread, and blessed, and broke

---

[12] Cf. Exod. 12:1-14.
[13] Luke 22:15.

it, and gave it to them, and said, 'Take; this is my Body.' And He took a cup, and when He had given thanks He gave it to them, and they all drank of it. And He said to them, 'This is my Blood of the covenant, which is poured out for many.' "[14]

∞

Christ gives priests the power of consecration

Jesus Himself performed the first Consecration at the Last Supper. He could perform this miracle — more wonderful than the creation of the world — because, as God, He is almighty. Now, by the will of Christ, His priests perform the miracle of changing bread and wine into the Body and Blood of Christ each time they offer Mass, because they have received that wondrous power from Him. Ever living in His Church, the Savior performs the miracle of Consecration over and over by associating with Himself a man whom He has consecrated and made His priest. He makes use of the voice of this man, of his heart — marked with the image of the Heart of Christ in the holy priesthood — and of his consecrated hands.

At the Last Supper, when Jesus said, "Do this in remembrance of me,"[15] He meant, "Do as you have seen and heard me do. I have changed bread and wine; so you also should change bread and wine. I have offered my Body and Blood in sacrifice; you, too, should do the same. I have given my Flesh and Blood in Holy Communion; so you also should give my Flesh and Blood to the faithful as nourishment for their souls." With this command, Jesus gave the Apostles and their successors — and them alone — the power to do what He had done, for without power they could not fulfill His command.

After the Savior had left them, the Apostles faithfully did what Jesus had commanded and empowered them to do. They changed bread and wine into Christ's Body and Blood, thus offering the

[14] Mark 14:22-24.
[15] Luke 22:19.

eucharistic Sacrifice in holy Mass, and gave Holy Communion to the faithful. Jesus had willed to leave a memorial of Himself not only to the Apostles but to all who were to believe in Him and love Him. His last will and testament was made for all time. The Apostles, knowing the purpose Jesus had in mind, continued to ordain worthy men to be bishops and priests and conferred upon them the power of consecration.

The two greatest powers of priests are those by which they forgive sins and change bread and wine into the Body and Blood of Christ. Just as the power to forgive sins would be needed in all generations, and so was transmitted to others by the Apostles, who were the first bishops of the Church, and handed on again by their successors as bishops, so has the power to consecrate bread and wine into the Body and Blood of Christ been transmitted to priests down through the generations. Jesus promised, "Lo, I am with you always, to the close of the age."[16]

The priest exercises the power to consecrate bread and wine into the Body and Blood of Christ only during the Mass. He himself can never grasp the sublimity of this power. He calls God back to earth again because through him the Incarnation has once again been renewed. He actually holds the Creator in his hands.

The Church has always believed and taught that through holy Ordination the priest obtains the mighty power that puts him on the level with the Apostles to whom Christ said, "Do this in remembrance of me." They exercise the power of consecration only "in the person of Christ Himself."

∞

The bread and wine become Christ's Body and Blood
When Jesus, the Son of God, said, "This is my Body. . . . This is my Blood," the bread became His Body, and the wine His Blood.

[16] Matt. 28:20.

Jesus said just what He meant and meant just what He said. This was the night before His death. He was solemnly dictating His last will and testament. He was using the dearest, simplest, most unmistakable words, not figurative or vague words.

St. John Damascene[17] wrote, "The bread and the wine are not merely figures of the Body and Blood of Christ (God forbid!) but the deified Body of the Lord itself, for the Lord has said, 'This is my Body,' not, 'This is a figure of my Body'; and 'my Blood,' not "a figure of my Blood.' "

Thus Jesus prepared the people by His promise of the Eucharist. If at the Last Supper He used those words — which not only Matthew, but Luke, Mark, and Paul say He spoke[18] — unless He meant what He said, He deliberately led astray the Apostles and His whole Church.

This was the teaching of the Church for fifteen centuries. In the sixteenth century, during the Protestant Reformation, a doctrine was introduced which denied that Christ meant what He said, but claimed that He intended something altogether different. Protestants are not agreed on just what He meant. If the Protestant interpretation were true, then for fifteen hundred years the "gates of Hell" — terrible error — prevailed against the Church that Jesus founded, in spite of His solemn promise to the contrary.[19] It would mean that for over nineteen hundred years, right up to the present time, the vast majority of all Christians, including all Roman Catholics, the Orthodox Church, and others, have been deceived by Christ.

Protestant churches generally interpret Christ's word to mean not "This is really my Body," but something like "This represents

---

[17] St. John Damascene (c. 675-c. 749), Greek theologian and Doctor of the Church.

[18] Cf. Matt. 26:26, 28; Mark 14:22, 24; Luke 22:19-20; 1 Cor. 11:24-25.

[19] Cf. Matt. 16:18.

me" or "The repetition of this action will remind you of me." Some hold that at the moment of Communion only, while the bread and wine are still present, Christ, too, is present by faith, together with the bread and wine. But great violence must be done to the texts in order to get these meanings, which our Lord never intended.

The Apostles and the early Christians understood the words spoken by Jesus at the Last Supper as He really meant them — that is, in the literal sense. St. Paul, referring to the drinking of the consecrated wine, which was common in those days, and the eating of the consecrated bread says, "The cup of blessing which we bless, is it not a participation in the Blood of Christ? The bread which we break, is it not a participation in the Body of Christ?"[20] Lest there be any doubt that he was referring to Holy Communion as the real and actual Body and Blood of Christ, he says, "Whoever, therefore, eats the bread or drinks the cup of the Lord in an unworthy manner will be guilty of profaning the Body and Blood of the Lord. . . . For anyone who eats and drinks without discerning the Body eats and drinks judgment upon himself."[21]

It is a historical fact that all Christians accepted the Eucharist in the same way that St. Paul did and with the same faith that the Catholic Church has taught from the time of Christ to the present, until the "Reformers" of the sixteenth century called the doctrine into question. The Orthodox Church, which broke away from Rome nine hundred years ago, and which has today over a hundred million members, has always taught and still teaches the same eucharistic doctrine as that of the Roman Catholic Church. For the past four hundred years, many Christians who claim to be guided by the Bible alone have been in disagreement with the plain teaching of Scripture.

[20] 1 Cor. 10:16.
[21] 1 Cor. 11:27, 29.

And yet Martin Luther once made this statement: "I wish that someone could convince me that in the Eucharist there is nothing more than bread and wine. I have thought of this question till the sweat has poured from my brow, and I confess I am still held in its bonds, and I see no way to free myself. The Gospel testimony is too clear."

Even Luther could not find a way to twist the clear words of our Lord. But His followers have succeeded in doing so, because they have discarded the truth of the Real Presence of Christ in the Blessed Sacrament.

At the Consecration, the bread and wine are changed into the Body and Blood of Christ; we know this only by faith in Jesus Christ, God Himself, who is able to do anything He wills, but cannot deceive us.

Some Protestants once asked Daniel O'Connell, the liberator of Ireland, how he could be so narrow-minded as to believe that Jesus Christ is truly present in the Eucharist. This faithful son of the Church answered without hesitation, "You'll have to discuss that with Jesus Christ Himself. He said so; therefore, I believe. If it is not true, He is to blame; but the truth of the Lord remains forever!"

When our Lord said, "This is my Body," the entire substance of the bread was changed into His Body; and when He said, "This is my Blood," the entire substance of the wine was changed into His Blood.

We say that the Holy Eucharist "really and truly" contains our Lord in order to point out the difference between the Catholic doctrine and the belief of most Protestants, who say that our Lord is present in this sacrament only figuratively, so that the Eucharist is only bread and wine representing the Body and Blood of Christ. But Jesus said, "This is my Body," not, "This is a sign of my Body." Hence His words pointed to His Real Presence, and they are to be taken in their literal sense.

Underneath all the appearances of a thing there is some reality — something that cannot be perceived by the senses — that causes the object to be what it is. When Jesus, referring to what was bread, said, "This is my Body," the appearance, or accidentals, remained there unchanged; but the substance of the bread was displaced by the substance of the Body of Christ, which existed thereafter under the appearance of bread. This change from the substance of bread into the substance of the Body of Christ is called "transubstantiation."

Only the appearance of the bread remained after Christ said the words of consecration. The object looked the same, felt the same, and tasted the same as before. Only the substance was changed. The senses only report what they see. They are not qualified, either before or after the words of consecration have been said, to judge what the object is. A Catholic is not expected to believe, contrary to the testimony of his senses, that the consecrated bread has come to look like the Flesh of Jesus or that the consecrated wine has come to look like His Blood. He is required to believe only that the imperceptible substance of the bread and wine has changed.

Our Lord is present whole and entire even in the smallest portion of the Holy Eucharist under the appearance of either bread or wine, just as our soul is present whole and entire in the smallest portion of our body. Jesus remains present in the Holy Eucharist as long as the appearances of bread and wine remain.

Christ's Body is present in the Eucharist in a way somewhat similar to the way in which the soul is in the body. The soul is present whole and entire in every portion of the living body. So the Body of Christ is present, whole and entire, in each part of the consecrated Host, both before and after the Host is broken.

When the priest breaks or divides the sacred Host, he breaks or divides the species only; the entire and living Body of Jesus Christ is present in each part.

Suppose a mother cuts a loaf of bread and gives a piece to each of her three children. The three portions are smaller than the whole loaf, but each child has bread. When the priest breaks the sacred Host, the parts are indeed small, but each part is the Body of Christ.

Suppose you see your face in a mirror. If you break the mirror into three pieces, you see your face in each of the three portions. If you join the three portions together, you see your face again, but only once. Christ is wholly and entirely present in the whole Host. When the priest breaks the Host into three parts, Christ is present whole and entire in each of the particles. At Holy Communion, the priest receives under two kinds, but he receives Christ only once.

In nature, too, we observe what appears to be the change of one substance into another. A person eats food, which is changed into the quite different substance of his body. If, then, through the wonderful process of digestion, we ourselves can change one substance into another, why should we question the power of God to make a substantial change directly?

The presence of Jesus in the Eucharist is true, actual, and miraculous. He can be here and in Heaven and in a thousand places. To the outward senses, He willed to be but a little piece of bread, at the same time living in all the completeness and beauty of His sacred humanity. He makes Himself so small that a child's hand can hold Him, and yet even Heaven itself cannot contain Him. Only His love and His power could work such wonders.

∞

Faith enables you to believe the mystery of the Eucharist

Faith is the first step in our union with Jesus. Through our understanding, we acknowledge and hold as true His revelation of Himself as God, our highest good and our last end. Jesus pointed out the motives for this union with Him by faith. He declared that

He is God, that He has worked miracles, and that we must hold fast to Him by faith if we wish to bring forth fruit unto eternal life. "Believe in God, believe also in me. . . . He who has seen me has seen the Father. . . . Do you not believe that I am in the Father and the Father in me? . . . Or else believe me for the sake of the works themselves. Truly, truly, I say to you, he who believes in me will also do the works that I do; and greater works than these will he do."[22] "He who abides in me, and I in him, he it is that bears much fruit, for apart from me you can do nothing. If a man does not abide in me, he is cast forth as a branch and withers."[23]

The Eucharist is called a *mystery of Faith*. A mystery is something that is known to be true, although it cannot be fully comprehended and may even have to be accepted on the word of another. Nature is full of mysteries, such as heat, light, and electricity.

The Consecration is a mystery. We cannot understand it, and we ought to avoid being too curious. In the *Imitation of Christ*, we read, "He that is a searcher into majesty shall be overwhelmed by its glory. Go forward, therefore, with simple and undoubting faith, and, with the reverence of a supplicant, approach this sacrament; and whatsoever thou art not able to understand, leave without care to Almighty God."[24]

Jesus wants us to believe firmly in His presence in the Holy Eucharist and thus merit a reward for our undoubting faith. The Apostle Thomas, who was unwilling to believe in the Resurrection of our Lord, said, "Unless I see in His hands the print of the nails, and place my finger in the mark of the nails, and place my hand in His side, I will not believe." After eight days, when Jesus again appeared to His Apostles, He said to Thomas, "Put your

---

[22] John 14:1, 9, 10-12.

[23] John 15:5-6.

[24] St. Thomas à Kempis (c. 1380-1471; ascetical writer), *Imitation of Christ*, Bk. 4, ch. 18, no. 1, 4.

finger here, and see my hands; and put out your hand, and place it in my side; do not be faithless, but believing." Thomas replied, "My Lord and my God!" The Savior then admonished him, "Have you believed because you have seen me? Blessed are those who have not seen and yet believe."[25]

Faith does not mean believing what we see and understand. The faith that one day will be rewarded in Heaven is the readiness to believe what we do not see and do not understand.

Furthermore, Jesus wants us to come to Him with childlike confidence. Jesus is now glorified. If He were to appear in all His glory, our eyes would be blinded by His majesty. Our Lord does not want us to come to Him in fear and trembling; He would have us speak to Him as a friend converses with a friend.

There is no action in which your faith can be exercised with greater intensity than in the Eucharist. There is no more sublime homage of faith than to believe in Christ, whose divinity and humanity are both hidden under the appearance of the Host. When Jesus, in showing you a little bread and wine, tells you, "This is my Body. . . . This is my Blood," and your intelligence, putting aside all that your senses say, accepts these words of Christ; when your will leads you in faith and love to the Holy Table, then you accomplish the highest act of faith that can be.

You have Christ's word for it that you may receive Him as a friendly Visitor in Holy Communion even every day. You can listen to Him as He speaks to you heart to heart, and you can speak with Him. You cannot see Him with your bodily eyes; but He tells you He is there, and all the more credit is due to you if you take Him at His word. It is for the great store of merit you can win that God has decreed that before you may see Christ face-to-face, you must carry on for a time just believing in Him and modeling your life on His life.

[25] John 20:25, 27-28, 29.

Chapter Two

✌

Adore Christ in the Eucharist

The continual presence of Jesus Christ here on earth is one of the effects of the Eucharist. The Savior is present on the altar during holy Mass from the Consecration to the Communion inclusively. St. John Chrysostom,[26] whom the Church honors as the "Doctor of the Eucharist," writes, "That which is in the chalice is the same as that which flowed from the side of Christ, and of this we are made partakers. . . . The wise men adored this Body when it lay in the manger; they prostrated themselves before it in fear and trembling. Now you behold the same Body which the wise men adored in the manger, lying upon the altar; you also know its power and salutary effect. . . . Already in the present life this mystery changes the earth for you into Heaven. The sublimest thing that is there — the Body of the Lord — you can behold here on earth. Yes, you not only behold it, but you touch it and eat it."

The sacrament and sacrifice of the Eucharist are inseparable. The Real Presence of Christ in the Host is the necessary and immediate consequence of transubstantiation. But the purpose of transubstantiation is first of all to make Christ present on the altar in a state of sacrifice by the separate consecration of bread and

---

[26] St. John Chrysostom (c. 347-407), Bishop of Constantinople.

wine. At the same time, the sacrifice cannot be completed without these consecrated species being received in Communion at least by the celebrating priest. What we adore in our visits to the Blessed Sacrament is Jesus Christ Himself, permanently present in the Host that was consecrated in the Holy Sacrifice and that will eventually be received in Communion.

Faith teaches us that Jesus Christ is truly, really, and essentially present, Body and Soul, divinity and humanity, under the veil of the sacramental species, so long as these species continue to exist. The Blessed Sacrament is therefore like a link that joins Heaven and earth in an essential union.

Jesus gave us the Holy Eucharist to remain ever on our altars as a proof of His love for us and to be worshiped by us. The Council of Trent says, "There is no room to doubt that all the faithful of Christ may, according to the custom ever received in the Catholic Church, render in veneration the worship which is due to the true God to this most holy Sacrament. . . . For we believe that same God to be present therein, of whom the eternal Father, when introducing Him into the world, says, 'And let all the angels of God adore Him'; whom the Magi falling down, adored; who, in fine, as the Scripture testifies, was adored by the Apostles in Galilee."

Under the appearance of bread are present our Lord's Blood and Soul as well as His Body, and under the appearance of wine are present His Body and Soul as well as His Blood, because in the Holy Eucharist are present the Body and Blood of the glorified Christ, who is in Heaven. In Heaven the Body, Blood, and Soul of Christ are inseparably united. The divinity of Christ is present both under the appearance of bread and under the appearance of wine, because from the time of the Incarnation, the divinity has been constantly and inseparably united to the entire human nature of Christ.

The Real Presence of Jesus in the Eucharist should awaken a return of love in your heart. How small a place Christ takes among us! How little He asks of you — only that you adore Him and receive Him as your food. The rest He leaves to your love and generosity. He accepts only as much outward honor as you bestow upon Him.

Once, when Jesus was on earth, men had to seek Him. Now He seeks men in order that He might make them happy — not only by His presence, but by the many blessings for soul and body that come with that presence.

∞

Adoration dates back to the early Church

In the early Church, the adoration of the Blessed Sacrament was restricted chiefly to the Mass and Holy Communion. Gradually, however, after the faithful were permitted to receive Holy Communion outside the Mass, many new and touching forms of adoration were permitted.

The teaching concerning the Real Presence of the eucharistic Christ is of supreme importance for the whole life of the Church, especially for her public worship. The Council of Trent teaches that the custom of reserving the Holy Eucharist is very ancient in the Catholic Church, as is the custom of bringing the Eucharist to the sick, and carefully reserving it for this purpose in churches. Church history tells us that in the early days the faithful frequently carried the Blessed Eucharist home or took it with them when they traveled, a custom that continued in some places until the twelfth century. The deacons were accustomed to bringing the Blessed Sacrament to those who were unable to attend Mass, as well as to prisoners and to the infirm.

Call to mind the history of the pagan priestess Domna in Nicomedia, who had been converted to Christianity by reading the Acts of the Apostles. When a cruel persecution broke out under Diocletian, Domna and her servant Indes were denounced to the heathen judge. He came to search her home but found only a copy of the Acts, a crucifix, a censer, a lamp, and a wooden case, or pyx, for the Blessed Sacrament. Do not these objects clearly point to the incense and sanctuary lamp — in a word, to the adoration of the Blessed Sacrament in the third century of the Church?

St. Gregory Nazianzen[27] in the fourth century relates of his sister, St. Corgonia, that when attacked by a mortal illness, she arose from her couch at night, prostrated herself before the altar, and invoked Him who is worshiped there in the Sacred Host, and obtained an instantaneous cure.

From the time of Emperor Constantine,[28] it was the general rule to reserve the Blessed Eucharist permanently in public churches. Can we imagine that, in these ages of faith, adoration of the eucharistic God should have ceased when the Church emerged from the catacombs? Listen to the witnesses of tradition, the Fathers of the Church: St. Augustine teaches, "No one eats the Flesh (the Body of our Lord) without first adoring it; yes, it would be a sin not to adore." St. John Chrysostom writes, "The Magi came from the uttermost ends of Persia to the stable, to visit and adore the Child; and we, who need not expose ourselves to the hardships of a long, wearisome journey, in order to be able to adore it in our churches and tabernacles, we who need only leave our houses, refuse to do this? Is this not the grossest negligence, yes, the most atrocious and blackest ingratitude?" What are these words but a fervent exhortation to visit our eucharistic Lord and an eloquent outburst of indignation at the neglect of this sacred practice?

The fourth canon of the Council of Tours, held in 567, indicates that the sanctuary gates were to remain open so that the faithful might at any time go before the altar for prayer. Among the collections of sacred anecdotes made by St. Gregory of Tours,[29] nothing

---

[27] St. Gregory Nazianzen (329-389), Bishop of Nazianzus.

[28] Constantine the Great (d. 337), Roman emperor.

[29] St. Gregory of Tours (c. 540-594), Bishop of Tours.

is more common than the expression "prostrate before the holy altar." Before the altar was the favorite place for every earnest prayer; the faithful knew that the Blessed Sacrament was reserved there — the Body of Christ, ever united to His Soul and divinity.

The Anglo-Saxons gave the highest worship to that which the ciborium or pyx contained. They called it "the adorable Host of the Son of God." They gave every sign of outward reverence to the church that contained it and to the altar on which it was offered.

Even Perpetual Adoration was practiced in those ages of faith. Pious cenobites in the East in the fifth century had consecrated themselves as a guard of perpetual honor to the divine King. Dividing themselves into different tribes, as the children of Israel of old, they sang psalms and prayed in the temple uninterruptedly. In the West, history proves that such Perpetual Adoration was observed in the monastery of Agaunum in the year 522.

St. Benedict[30] and his monks, by clearing the forests, draining the marshes, and erecting magnificent churches where the Lord dwelt under the eucharistic veils, were the pioneer missionaries and Apostles of the Most Blessed Sacrament and brought the barbaric hordes to the Faith, making them fervent adorers of the hidden God of the Eucharist.

After the tenth century, devotion to the Blessed Sacrament received an extraordinary impetus. The institution of the glorious feast of Corpus Christi by Pope Urban IV in 1246, at the suggestion of Blessed Juliana of Liège, who in various visions had been instructed to request the introduction of this feast, caused an outburst of enthusiasm. For this feast, the great St. Thomas Aquinas composed admirable hymns.[31] This new festival became the first

---

[30] St. Benedict (c. 480-c. 550), father of Western monasticism.

[31] Cf. St. Thomas Aquinas (c. 1225-1274; Dominican philosopher, theologian, and Doctor of the Church), *The Aquinas Prayer Book*, trans. Robert Anderson and Johann Moser (Manchester, New Hampshire: Sophia Institute Press, 2000).

golden link of that glorious chain of public adoration and splendid devotions and triumphal processions and numberless visits that extends through the centuries down to our day.

At this period we find in convents and monasteries of men and women the practice of visiting the Blessed Sacrament, of silent adoration of the Holy Eucharist, and of prayers poured out before the altar.

Both St. Thomas More and St. John Fisher[32] were strengthened in life and prepared themselves for a holy death and martyrdom by fervent adoration of the Blessed Sacrament. A prayer of St. Thomas More has fortunately been preserved, in which occur the following words:

> O sweet Savior Christ,
> by the diverse torments of Thy most bitter Passion,
> take from me, good Lord, this lukewarm fashion
> or rather key-cold manner of meditation,
> and this dullness in praying to Thee.
> And give me Thy grace to long for Thy Holy Sacraments,
> and especially to rejoice in the presence of Thy blessed Body,
> sweet Savior Christ, in the Holy Sacrament of the Altar,
> and duly to thank Thee for Thy gracious visitation therewith.

St. Bonaventure,[33] the Seraphic Doctor, was in the habit of going to the foot of the tabernacle to draw the wisdom and holiness that adorned his life; and in this he was a faithful disciple of his humble Father and Founder, St. Francis of Assisi,[34] who used to go to communicate all his labors and undertakings to Jesus in the

---

[32] St. Thomas More (1478-1535), Lord Chancellor of England, and St. John Fisher (1469-1535), Bishop of Rochester, were martyred under Henry VIII.

[33] St. Bonaventure (c. 1217-1274), Franciscan theologian.

[34] St. Francis of Assisi (1182-1226), founder of the Franciscan Order.

Most Holy Sacrament. St. Clare,[35] the great associate of St. Francis of Assisi, cherished visits to the Blessed Sacrament above all others and most earnestly recommended them to her spiritual daughters, the Poor Clares.

The Angelic Doctor, St. Thomas Aquinas, is said to have imbibed his heavenly wisdom from the crucifix and the tabernacle, where he spent hours together; and in this he but reflected the spirit of his order and of his illustrious father, St. Dominic.[36]

From the sixteenth to the twentieth century, four factors contributed to the growth and development of the adoration of the Blessed Sacrament and of the practice of the daily visits.

The first factor was the fierce onslaught that the Protestant Reformers made upon these sacred practices of the Church. The Church defined the true Catholic doctrine and practice in the Council of Trent. Then her children were spurred on by faith and love to make reparation for doctrinal abuses by fervent adoration and visits to the eucharistic God.

The second factor was the institution of the Forty Hours' Devotion.[37] Father Joseph, a Capuchin of Milan, is now generally said to be the first to celebrate the Forty Hours' Devotion in the year 1534. The devotion was soon taken up by St. Philip Neri[38] and others in Rome and by St. Charles Borromeo[39] in Milan, and, as early as 1692, Pope Clement VIII prescribed it for Rome.

The third factor was the establishment of orders, houses, and confraternities of Perpetual Adoration as it is practiced in our

---

[35] St. Clare (1194-1253), foundress of the Poor Clares.

[36] St. Dominic (1170-1221), founder of the Order of Friars Preachers.

[37] A devotion in which the Blessed Sacrament is exposed for forty hours for adoration by the faithful.

[38] St. Philip Neri (1515-1595), Italian priest who founded the Congregation of the Oratory.

[39] St. Charles Borromeo (1538-1584), Archbishop of Milan.

own day. Sister Mechtildis of the Blessed Sacrament in 1652 founded the Congregation of the Benedictine Nuns of the Perpetual Adoration.

The fourth factor was the life and influence of Pope St. Pius X.[40] In the address at his canonization, May 29, 1954, Pope Pius XII said, "A priest, above all in the eucharistic ministry: this is the most faithful portrayal of St. Pius X. To serve the mystery of the Blessed Eucharist as a priest, and to fulfill the command of our Savior — 'Do this in remembrance of me' — was his goal. From the day of his sacred Ordination until his death as Pope, he knew no other path than this in order to arrive at heroism and in his love of God and to bring about a wholehearted return to that Redeemer of the world, who by means of the Blessed Eucharist poured out the wealth of His divine love on men. His deep awareness of his priesthood was clearly demonstrated by the extreme care he took to renew the dignity of divine worship. Overcoming the prejudices springing from an erroneous practice, he resolutely promoted frequent, and even daily, Communion of the faithful, and unhesitatingly led children to the banquet of the Lord, offering them to the embrace of the God hidden on the altars. The spouse of Christ experienced a new springtime of eucharistic life.

"The Holy Eucharist and the interior life: this is the supreme Adoration of the Real Presence and universal lesson which St. Pius X, from the height of glory, teaches in this hour to all souls. As apostle of the interior life, he becomes, in the age of machine and organization, the saint and guide of men of our time."

∝∞

In the Eucharist, Christ lets you approach Him
After His mortal course on earth had ended, Jesus desired to return to His Father, but without leaving us. How marvelously His

---

[40] St. Pius X (1835-1914), Pope from 1903.

divine wisdom brought this about in the Holy Sacrament of the Altar! If He had remained in the splendor of His glorified body, our eyes would not have been able to bear it, and we would not have dared to approach Him. In the Eucharist He covers His splendor with the sacramental veils. He might have veiled Himself beneath other appearances; but He preferred the appearance of bread to make us understand that He is the "Bread of God . . . come down from Heaven, which gives life to the world"[41] by divinely nourishing our souls. To the appearance of bread He added the appearance of wine to make us understand that the Eucharist is a complete banquet and that Mass is the Sacrifice of Calvary continued.

How eager Jesus is to be with us! He does not dwell in one temple only, as at Jerusalem, but within reach of all. He does not withdraw into the innermost court, as formerly, where none but the highest priest, once a year, might approach Him; He does not demand a splendid building for His home. The Jews had the tables of the Law in their tabernacle, surrounded by the visible glory of God; but we have Jesus, the very Author of the Law, in our tabernacle, who with the Father and the Holy Spirit is the infinite Being, the Almighty, the Creator of all things — veiling the glory of God out of compassion, because it is too great for man to see and live.

In order to give Himself to us, He hides Himself, no longer under the veils of mortal flesh, but under the appearances of bread and wine. He descends from His throne in Heaven to dwell in poverty and to be worshiped in simplicity, so that He may be visited by all and give Himself even to the poorest sinner. He lays aside even the dignity of man and becomes in appearance helpless, entirely at the disposal of man. It is His delight to be with the children of men.[42] What wealth is hidden beneath the thin, white veils of bread! The Sacred Host appears so frail and small,

---

[41] Cf. John 6:33.
[42] Cf. Prov. 8:31.

yet in its sacred sanctuary we see with eyes of faith our very God, our hidden God!

∾

Jesus abides with us in the Eucharist

In the Holy Eucharist, Jesus becomes present not only to renew the Sacrifice of Calvary in an unbloody manner on our altars and nourish our souls in Holy Communion, but also to abide bodily among us by His Real Presence in our tabernacles.

Jesus remains in the tabernacle day and night, not idle, but full of life and continual action. He is always in loving adoration before His heavenly Father, taking delight in thinking how lovable and great the Father is in Himself and honoring Him by His humble life in the Eucharist. Sublime is the honor Jesus renders Him there in the tabernacle at all times, because He never interrupts it during a single moment of the day or night, and in all places. It is of infinite value because it is offered by the very Son of God.

Jesus occupies Himself at the same time with your dearest interests. He thanks God for you, prays continually for you, asks pardon for your sins, and makes reparation and amends for them. He is always offering Himself in sacrifice to God and continually pouring out His graces upon all mankind as a eucharistic Mediator.

The Holy Eucharist continues the life of Jesus among us. Every day He is born again in a state that is similar to that of the Incarnation. He comes upon the altar as God and man at the word of a priest, is laid in his consecrated hands and wrapped in the pure, white swaddling clothes of the appearance of bread.

Jesus renews His hidden life in the deep stillness and concealment by which He veils even His human nature; in the poverty in which He lives in the tabernacle; in His obedience to His priests; and in His quiet and unseen work in souls.

He renews His public life by His presence everywhere in the world as Teacher, Healer, and Friend. How many miracles are worked in the souls of men through holy Mass and Communion! How many souls are taught, blessed, comforted, and healed! In Palestine He was in one place only; now He is everywhere, ready to assist all. He is here, the Son of God with all His divine power and infinite love, to radiate His sacred influence upon our souls and upon the world, to draw all mankind, to be the source of all strength, life, and joy.

The mysteries of His Passion are contained in the Eucharist, for it is a remembrance of His death. Holy Mass is a repetition of the Sacrifice of the Last Supper and the Sacrifice of the Cross. How often is the Eucharist also the renewal of His sufferings! The sacrileges, forgetfulness, and disrespect that He receives must wound His Heart, which has always been on fire with love for men; He felt it all when He knelt in the Garden of Gethsemane and when He hung on the Cross. His repose in the tabernacle reminds us of His rest in the sepulcher.

The glory of His risen life also is renewed in the Eucharist. He is present here in His glorious, transfigured Body, just as He appeared after His Resurrection. He abides with us as He did with the Apostles. He makes Himself the friendly Companion of our pilgrimage, as He did to the travelers on their way to Emmaus.[43] He watches us from the quiet tabernacle while we go on through life, comforting and encouraging, blessing our work, unsuccessful though it appears, as He blessed Peter's fishing.[44]

All these mysteries of the life of Jesus are renewed in the Holy Eucharist for the benefit of our soul. In the tabernacle are Bethlehem, Nazareth, Mount Tabor, Calvary, and Heaven itself. "Behold, the dwelling of God is with men. He will dwell with them."[45] On our altars is Jesus in the Holy Eucharist, easy for all to find,

---

[43] Cf. Luke 24:13 ff.
[44] Cf. John 21:6.
[45] Rev. 21:3.

ready to help and to converse in loving intimacy with all His children. From the eucharistic throne, streams of light and power, of joy and peace, of comfort and blessing, pour into countless human hearts that come to Him with confidence, humility, and earnest love, in times of trouble and need.

∞

Model your life on the eucharistic Lord

In the Blessed Sacrament, Jesus is your model of a perfect life, your way to your home in Heaven. His presence among us teaches us many virtues that you must practice, the greatest of which is charity toward God and men. You can unite your acts of devotion with that perfect adoration, thanksgiving, atonement, and prayer that He offers to God without ceasing in the Holy Sacrament as an expression of His tender love for Him. It is only through Jesus, with Jesus, and in Jesus that God is known, honored, and glorified as He rightly deserves to be.

You can join your acts of charity toward your fellowmen with the devoted love and continual care that He shows by sacrificing Himself for them, by assisting them in their needs, and by praying earnestly for their salvation.

Here He leaves Himself entirely to the disposal of men. With what *patience* He bears with their coldness, irreverence, and negligence! He returns their ingratitude with kindly love.

With what perfect *obedience* He becomes present on our altars during holy Mass at the simple words of a priest!

You could not have a more beautiful model of *humility* than Jesus in the Blessed Sacrament. Glorious as is His risen Body, sublime as is His divinity, the eucharistic veil covers everything. He rules the world in the secret stillness of the tabernacle. He is in truth a hidden God.

In the Blessed Sacrament, He exhorts you to *chastity*. By giving you His virginal Flesh in Holy Communion, He makes your body the temple and your soul the sanctuary of the infinitely holy God. The beauty of the sacred vessels and the whiteness of the altar linens remind you of the purity with which you should receive His most sacred Body.

He teaches you *poverty,* for He is satisfied with the humble covering of the bread and wine, even lessening Himself within the limits of a tiny particle.

God gives His grace to those who are sincere and humble. It is at Holy Communion and at prayer, especially before the Blessed Sacrament, that you will receive the greatest and most abundant graces from God, for Jesus in the Eucharist is not only your Model in practicing virtue, but also the source of all the graces you need. Endeavor to imitate Him.

Chapter Three

∽

Visit Jesus in the Blessed Sacrament

Our Lord's last will is expressed in His words spoken shortly before He began His Sacred Passion: "Abide in me, and I in you. As the branch cannot bear fruit by itself, unless it abides in the vine, neither can you, unless you abide in me."[46] This union with Christ is made perfect in Holy Communion. Hence Holy Communion is God's best means of sanctifying you.

But you may remain closely united with Jesus even after Holy Communion. The act of Communion is passing, but the effect it produces — namely, union with Christ — is meant to be permanent. Jesus does not dwell with you by His bodily presence, yet He does so by the outpourings of His love, by the lights and graces He sends you without ceasing from the tabernacle.

St. Mary Magdalene de' Pazzi[47] wrote, "A friend will visit his friend in the morning to wish him a good day, in the evening, a good night, taking also an opportunity to converse with him during the day. In like manner, make visits to Jesus Christ in the Blessed Sacrament, if your duties permit it. It is especially at the foot of the altar that one prays well. In all your visits to our Savior,

---

[46] John 15:4.

[47] St. Mary Magdalene de' Pazzi (1566-1607), Carmelite mystic.

frequently offer His Precious Blood to the eternal Father. You will find these visits very conducive to increase in you divine love."

It is by visits to the Blessed Sacrament that you open your soul to His transforming action. Share with Him your joys and sorrows, your feelings and affections, your plans and desires. Your whole life is meant to be a sharing with Christ, gradually transforming you into Christ. This is the marvelous effect of prayer before the tabernacle.

Jesus wishes to be your Friend in the Blessed Sacrament. There is always something lacking in friendship that is only human. You need His divine friendship, for there are times when you are very much alone, when everyone seems weary of you, when you are discouraged. But Christ is close to you in the tabernacle as your best Friend, as your Companion in exile, with a Heart human like your own; a Heart that can understand your sorrows and problems, since it has experienced all that you must bear. His Heart can sympathize with you and befriend you in your hour of need; He can love you with the love of the best of friends. Like a real furnace of love, His Heart burns all for you with a love that knows no end because it has its source in the depths of the Godhead — all for you, as if there were no other to share its infinite warmth. Not all the tender affection He pours out upon countless other souls lessens His love for you. Even when you forget Him, He thinks of you; even when you offend or disappoint Him, He sacrifices Himself for you at Mass; when you have trials, He is ready to console and strengthen you.

Your Savior has brought Heaven to earth by giving you Himself in the Most Blessed Sacrament, for He is the same God who is in Heaven, surrounded by His angels; and at the foot of the altar you may associate yourself with all the heavenly court who form an invisible guard around Him. You would deprive yourself of the sweetest joys of your life if you failed to come and pour out your love and petitions before His tabernacle. It is the true refuge of your soul, where you find comfort, guidance, strength, peace, sanctity, and happiness. Even though the burdens of your life seem almost unbearable at times, you have a Friend who will never fail: your God in the Holy Eucharist, imprisoned by His very love in the tabernacle. His Sacred Heart calls to you, too, from the tabernacle, "Come to me, all who labor and are heavy laden, and I will give you rest."[48]

How beautiful is the prayer of St. Bonaventure: "Draw me entirely into Your Heart, for Your side was pierced so that it might be open as an entrance to receive us. Your Heart was wounded so that we might abide in it and find relief in every trouble from without."

∞

The saints show devotion to the eucharistic Christ

The saints and truly devout souls have always made frequent visits to the Blessed Sacrament. St. Francis Xavier,[49] after spending the entire day laboring for the salvation of souls, would often spend the night in prayer before the Blessed Sacrament. When he was overcome by sleep, he would cast himself on the altar steps for a short rest and then continue his conversation with our divine Lord.

After a day of wearisome labor, St. John Francis Regis[50] found his rest before the tabernacle. And if he found the church already locked, he would kneel before the door.

St. Francis of Assisi never undertook any work without first going into the church to ask the blessing of Jesus. St. Mary Magdalene de' Pazzi made thirty visits to the Blessed Sacrament daily.

---

[48] Matt. 11:28.

[49] St. Francis Xavier (1506-1552), Jesuit missionary known as the Apostle of the Indies.

[50] St. John Francis Regis (1597-1640), Jesuit priest dedicated to serving the poor.

St. Alphonsus Liguori[51] loved the devotion of daily visits to the Blessed Sacrament most ardently. He leaves you the following recommendation: "Withdraw yourself from people and spend at least a quarter of an hour, or a half-hour, in some church in the presence of the Blessed Sacrament. Taste and see how sweet is the Lord. Try it, and you will learn from your own experience how many graces this will bring you. The time you spend devoutly before our eucharistic Lord will prove the most meritorious for you in this life; and it will be the greatest consolation for you at the hour of death and for all eternity. Be sure that you will probably gain more by praying for fifteen minutes before the Blessed Sacrament, than by all the other spiritual exercises of the day. True, our Lord hears our prayers anywhere, for He has made the promise, 'Ask, and you shall receive,' but He has revealed to His servants that those who visit Him in the Blessed Sacrament will obtain a more abundant measure of grace."

The Curé of Ars, St. John Vianney,[52] told his people, "Our Lord is hidden there in the tabernacle, waiting for us to come and visit Him, and make our requests to Him. See how good He is! He accommodates Himself to our weakness. In Heaven, where we shall be glorious and triumphant, we shall see Him in all His glory. If He had presented Himself before us in that glory now, we would not have dared to approach Him; but He hides Himself, like a person in a prison, who might say to us, 'You do not see me, but that is no matter; ask of me all you wish, and I will grant it.' Jesus is there to console us, and therefore we ought often to visit Him. How pleasing to Him is the short quarter of an hour that we steal from our occupations, from something of no use, to come and pray to Him, to visit Him, to console Him for all the outrages He receives!

---

[51] St. Alphonsus Liguori (1696-1787), moral theologian and founder of the Redemptorists.

[52] St. John Vianney (1786-1859), patron saint of parish priests.

What happiness do we not feel in the presence of God, when we find ourselves alone at His feet before the holy tabernacle!"

St. Thérèse of the Child Jesus wrote, "When deserted by creatures and in moments of sadness I would go up to the sanctuary of the chapel and find my only consolation in that silent visit. I remember that I often then repeated this line from a beautiful poem my father used to recite for us: Time is thy ship, and not thy dwelling place."

∞

Learn how to make visits to the Blessed Sacrament

In regard to the manner of making the daily visit, Father Faber aptly remarks, "The ways of visiting the Blessed Sacrament must be as various as the souls of men. Some love to go there to listen; some to speak; some to confess to Him as if He were their priest; some to examine their consciences as before their judge; some to do homage as to their king; some to study Him as their Doctor and Prophet; some to find shelter as with their Creator. Some rejoice in His divinity, others in His sacred humanity, others in the mysteries of the season. Some visit Him on different days by His different titles, as God, Father, Brother, Shepherd, Head of the Church, and the like. Some visit to adore, some to intercede, some to petition, some to return thanks, some to get consolation; but all visit Him to love."[53]

Whatever method you employ, your visit should abound in acts of thanksgiving, reparation, and petition. The devotion of the Blessed Sacrament is practically identified with the devotion to the Sacred Heart, which promotes frequent visits to the Blessed Sacrament and is in turn nourished by them. Your daily visits will become most pleasing to the Sacred Heart and profitable to yourself, if they are made with the express intention to thank Jesus for

[53] Frederick William Faber, *The Blessed Sacrament*.

the numberless blessings He bestows through the Eucharist and to make reparation to Him, for He remains for us day and night on our altars and is frequently abandoned.

The aim of your visits to the Blessed Sacrament should be to express your love for Jesus. Declare your faith in the Real Presence of Christ in the little white Host that contains His divinity and humanity, all the treasures of His Sacred Heart, all the kindness and goodness by which during His mortal life He made those who came near Him exceedingly happy.

Arouse in your heart the cheerful confidence of a child, and you will find in Jesus all that you need: forgiveness of your sins and of the punishments due to them; the grace never again to offend Him willfully and always to fight courageously against the weakness of nature and the attraction of evil; to do penance by prayer and work to the extent of your ability; to persevere to the end in doing good and, after a happy death, to inherit eternal joy. His fidelity never wavers; His wisdom, goodness, and power never fail.

You can present your very special petitions to the Savior when you attend a devotion at which the Blessed Sacrament is exposed, or at the moment of Benediction. Such favorite petitions might be for the remission of all guilt and punishment for the sins of your past life; for the grace never again to commit a deliberate sin, and, as far as possible, also lessen the number of your faults; that you may learn to seek only that which has value for eternity and not set your heart on worldly things; that from day to day you may become more like Christ; that you may follow all the inspirations of grace; that you may acquire a tender love for the Mother of God; or that you may be generous in prayer, labor, and penance. And think of the numerous petitions you may have to present on behalf of your family! At the sacramental blessing it is Jesus Himself who blesses you, and His blessing is as powerful and fruitful today as it was during His mortal life. Therefore, make the most of the opportunity!

Blessed Henry Suso[54] wrote, "The time that you pass with devotion at the foot of the altar before Jesus Christ is the time wherein you will obtain most graces, and which will be your greatest consolation at the hour of death and during eternity. There is no place where Jesus Christ hears our prayers more promptly."

Speak to Jesus as you would with your best friend who already knows all about your needs and problems and is the only one who can really help you. Tell Him about the work you are doing, pleasant or unpleasant, about your temptations, faults, difficulties, hopes, and worries.

In your visits to the Tabernacle, offer Jesus to the heavenly Father and offer yourself with Jesus. The constant attitude of Christ before His Father is that of offering Himself and of offering us. The constant attitude of the Christian before Christ is that of offering Him, and of offering himself with Jesus.

Our Lord unceasingly offers Himself to His Father and gives Him marvelous worship of thanks and adoration without limit. Every moment of the day, the Son of God offers Himself to the Father for the redemption of the world. More than 360,000 Masses are offered in twenty-four hours, or four elevations of the Eucharist each second. Each time your heart beats, and even more often, you can say Jesus is offering Himself. Devotion to the Eucharist includes the longing to offer to God through Jesus Christ in the Blessed Sacrament an infinite thanksgiving and reparation.

If a grace is granted to you, offer the divine Host as the only thanks worthy of God. If you fall into some sin, offer the Precious Blood in reparation. If you are suffering pain, unite your sacrifices to that of the holy Victim on the altar. Join yourself to the divine prayer of the Savior and plead for the Church, for the great interests of God in souls, for sinners, for the missions, for priests, and for your family.

---

[54] Blessed Henry Suso (c. 1295-1366), German mystic.

To offer Jesus to God means to offer the entire Christ — not only Jesus the Son of Mary, but every one of us who are members of His Mystical Body.[55] Christ sums up in Himself all of redeemed and faithful humanity, the whole Church, the society of saints. It is the complete Jesus who offers Himself to God. You are "part of Jesus Christ," and that explains how you can offer Jesus to the Father, and why you must offer yourself to the Father with Jesus.

St. Margaret Mary[56] once described her prayer thus: "I generally finish without any other request or offering than that of my Jesus to His eternal Father in this manner: My God, I offer Your well-beloved Son in thanksgiving for all the benefits You have conferred upon me, for my request, my offering, my adoration, all my resolutions, and finally I offer Him for my love and my all. Receive Him, eternal Father, for all that You wish of me, since I can offer You nothing worthy of You except Him whom You give me to enjoy with so much love."

---

[55] That is, the Church (cf. 1 Cor. 12:27; Col. 1:18).

[56] St. Margaret Mary Alacoque (1647-1690), Visitation nun and chief founder of devotion to the Sacred Heart of Jesus.

Chapter Four

∞

Let the Eucharist lead you to the Sacred Heart

Devotion to the Sacred Heart, as we now know it, began about the year 1672. On repeated occasions Jesus appeared to St. Margaret Mary, a Visitation nun in France, and during these apparitions He explained to her the devotion to His Sacred Heart as He wanted people to practice it. He asked to be honored in the figure or symbol of His Heart of flesh; He asked for acts of reparation, for frequent Communion, Communion on the first Friday of the month, and the keeping of the Holy Hour.

When the Catholic Church approved the devotion to the Sacred Heart of Jesus, she did not base her action merely on the visions of St. Margaret Mary. The Church approved the devotion on its own merits. We honor the Sacred Heart not only because every drop of Christ's Precious Blood passed through it during the thirty-three years of His life on earth; not only because the Sacred Heart throbbed in closest sympathy with every movement of joy or sorrow, pity or love in our best Friend, but we honor the Sacred Heart of Jesus because of its intimate union with His divinity. There is only one person in Jesus, and that person was at the same time God and man. Therefore every part of His body was human and divine. His Heart, too, is divine; it is the Heart of God.

Devotion to the Heart of Jesus alone, as a noble part of His sacred body, would not be devotion to the Sacred Heart as understood and approved by the Church. There are two things that must always be found together in the devotion to the Sacred Heart: Christ's Heart of flesh and Christ's love for us. True devotion to the Sacred Heart means devotion to the divine Heart of Christ insofar as this Heart represents and recalls His love for us. It means devotion to the love of Jesus Christ for us insofar as this love is recalled and represented to us by His Heart of flesh.

In his great encyclical letter on devotion to the Sacred Heart, Pope Pius XII explained the real nature of devotion to the most Sacred Heart of Jesus in the light of divine revelation, its chief source, and the graces that flow from it. He said, "We think that Our statements, confirmed by the teaching of the Gospel, have made it clear that essentially this devotion is nothing else than devotion to the human and divine love of the Incarnate Word and to the love which the Heavenly Father and the Holy Ghost have for sinful men. For, as the Angelic Doctor teaches, the first cause of man's redemption is the love of the August Trinity. This love, pouring forth abundantly into the human will of Jesus Christ and His Adorable Heart, moved Him to shed His Blood to redeem us from the captivity of sin."[57]

Devotion to the Sacred Heart bears something that is universal. In honoring the Heart of Christ, it is no longer on Jesus as infant, youth, or victim that our homage lingers but on the Person of Jesus in the fullness of His love.

Being directed to the love of Christ for us, our devotion to the Sacred Heart finds and sees in Jesus everything connected with His love for us. This love of Christ for us was the moving force of all He did and suffered for us — in the manger, on the Cross, in giving Himself in the Blessed Sacrament, in His teaching, in His

---

[57] *Haurietis Aquas* (May 15, 1956), sect. 89.

praying, and in His healing. So when we speak of the Sacred Heart, we mean Jesus showing us His Heart — Jesus all love for us and all lovable.

∞

Discover in the Eucharist Christ's love for you

The Heart of Jesus became in time the symbol of God's love for men. He loved men while on earth. He never ceases to love them in Heaven. Because He loves us, He sanctifies us through the sacraments. These are inexhaustible fountains of grace and holiness that have their source in the boundless ocean of the Sacred Heart of Jesus.

In the Eucharist especially Jesus gives us the greatest proof of His love. The Council of Trent says, "When our Savior was about to depart out of this world to the Father, He instituted this sacrament, in which He poured forth, as it were, the riches of His divine love toward man." The Holy Eucharist, therefore, is first and foremost the sacrament of God's love for man; for it contains the God-Man, Jesus Christ, whose Sacred Heart is a burning furnace of love. He is really present under the visible appearances of bread and wine, not only to enable us to offer Him in the Mass, and to come to Him, as friends visit a friend; He is there also that we may unite ourselves most intimately to Him. In the Holy Eucharist we become even more closely united to Jesus than the food we eat is united to our body. The power of His love makes us grow together with Him into one Mystical Body, sharing in His life and love. Thus the living union of the soul with God that began in Baptism and was strengthened in Confirmation is continued and made even more intimate in Holy Communion.

Pope Pius XII describes the love of the Sacred Heart of Jesus in giving us the Holy Eucharist in these words: "Who in truth could describe in a worthy manner those beatings of the Divine Heart, the indications of His infinite love, when He bestowed His greatest

43

gifts on man — that is, Himself in the sacrament of the Eucharist, His Most Holy Mother, and the priestly office communicated to us?

"Even before He ate the Last Supper with His disciples, when He knew that He was going to institute the sacrament of His Body and Blood by the shedding of which the new covenant was to be consecrated, He felt His Heart stirred by strong emotions, which He made known to the Apostles in these words: 'I have greatly desired to eat this Passover with you before I suffer' (Luke 22:15).

"These same emotions were even stronger, without doubt, when 'having taken bread, He gave thanks and broke it and gave it to them saying: This is my Body which is being given for you; do this in remembrance of me. In like manner, he took also the cup after the supper, saying: This cup is the new covenant in my Blood, which shall be shed for you' (Luke 22:19, 20).

"Rightly, therefore, one may affirm that the Divine Eucharist, both as a sacrament and as a sacrifice — the one He bestowed on men, the other He Himself continually offers 'from the rising of the sun even to the going down' (Mal. 1:11) — and the priesthood are all really the gifts of the Most Sacred Heart of Jesus."[58]

Because Jesus longs to be with His own, He instituted this Sacrament of Love, that by it He might abide with us. Since His presence is concealed by the Sacred Species, He does not want us to lose the merit of faith — the blessings promised to those who "have not seen and yet believe."[59]

Who could have conceived such a gift? Jesus utterly strips Himself of His glory, so that He may be accessible to us, whose feeble nature in its present condition could not gaze on His majesty and live. He accommodates Himself to our weakness because He loves us with an infinite love.

[58] *Haurietis Aquas*, sect. 70-71.
[59] John 20:29.

For twenty centuries, Jesus has been with us night and day, like a father who will not leave his children, like a friend who finds his pleasure with his friends, like a devoted physician who constantly remains by the bedside of his patients. He is ever active, adoring, praying, and glorifying His Father for us, thanking Him for all the benefits He continually bestows upon us, loving Him in our stead, offering Him His own merits and satisfactions to atone for our sins, and ever asking new graces on our behalf. As St. Paul says, "He is able for all time to save those who draw near to God through Him, since He always lives to make intercession for them."[60]

He never ceases to renew upon the altar the sacrifice of Calvary thousands of times a day, wherever there is a priest to consecrate the elements. He does so out of love for us, in order to apply to each one of us the fruits of His Holy Sacrifice. Not content with immolating Himself, He gives Himself whole and entire to everyone who wishes to receive Him in Holy Communion, to impart to each His graces and His virtues.

Let us follow the advice of St. Peter Canisius,[61] who writes, "In every trial take refuge with all earnestness in the loving Heart of Christ. Reflect on His goodness and love for you, and compare it with your own sinfulness, unfaithfulness, and unworthiness. How great is the love of Christ, who invites all to come to Him: 'Come to me, all who labor and are heavy laden, and I will give you rest.'

"He proves Himself willing and even desirous of sharing the cares of each and every one, because He loves all of us. Therefore, with great confidence cast your sins into the abyss of His love, and you will soon find relief."

Love could go no further than did the love of Jesus Christ when He died for us on the Cross. "Greater love has no man than this,

---

[60] Heb. 7:25.

[61] St. Peter Canisius (1521-1597), Jesuit theologian.

that a man lay down his life for his friends."[62] But the Son of God devised a yet more astonishing manner of expressing His love. He yearned to be most closely identified with us. He instituted the Holy Eucharist in order that He might come every day under the form of this life-giving Bread. The words of Scripture can most truly be applied to Him: "My delights were to be with the children of men."[63]

The Apostles must have asked Him at the Last Supper, "Master, what are we going to do when You are gone?" Jesus no doubt would have reassured them by saying, "I shall not leave you. My Sacred Heart will be with you in the Holy Eucharist. That Heart will mean everything in the world to you." He was also speaking of the Holy Eucharist when He spoke His last words before ascending into Heaven: "Behold, I am with you all days, even until the end of the world."[64]

Pope Pius XII again states, "Ardent devotion to the Heart of Jesus will without doubt encourage and promote devotion to the Most Holy Cross and love for the Most August Sacrament of the Altar. . . . Nor will it be easy to grasp the force of that love by which Christ was impelled to give us Himself as our spiritual food except by fostering a special devotion to the Eucharistic Heart of Jesus. The purpose of this devotion, to use the words of Our predecessor of happy memory, Leo XIII, is to recall to our minds 'that supreme act of love by which Our Redeemer, pouring forth all the riches of His Heart, instituted the adorable sacrament of the Eucharist to remain in our midst to the end of time.' For 'the Eucharist is not the smallest portion of His Heart which He gave us from the overflowing love of His Heart.' "[65]

---

[62] John 15:13.

[63] Prov. 8:31 (Douay-Rheims translation).

[64] Cf. Matt. 28:20.

[65] *Haurietis Aquas*, sect. 122.

Let the Eucharist lead you to the Sacred Heart

∞

Love Christ's Sacred Heart in the Eucharist

Devotion to the Sacred Heart in the Eucharist consists in two essential facts: love and atonement.

Love is the first and foremost of these duties. Love is the Lord's first and greatest commandment, the bond of perfection. God asks for our love because He wishes to be the God and Master of our hearts through love. Sacrifice is but a means to prove our love and loyalty. Our Lord has loved us with an infinite love, even unto death, and still loves us without limit. He wants to be loved by us. He appeals to our hearts and bids us love Him in return.

St. Margaret Mary writes, "He made me see that it was the great desire He had of being loved by men, and of withdrawing them from the road of perdition, that induced Him to conceive this plan of making His Heart known to men, with all the treasures of love, of mercy, of grace, of sanctification, and of salvation, in order that those who wish to render and procure Him all the honor, glory, and love of which they are capable, might be abundantly and profusely enriched with the treasures of the Heart of God."

In another letter, she writes, "Let us, then, love this, the only love of our souls, since He has loved us first and loves us still so ardently that He continually burns with love for us in the Blessed Sacrament. To become saints it suffices to love this Holy of Holies. What shall hinder us? We have hearts to love and a body to suffer. . . . Only His holy love can make us do His pleasure; only this perfect love can make us do it in His own way; and only this perfect love can make us do it in His own acceptable time."

This act of love is highly sanctifying. By uniting you intimately to the Sacred Heart of Jesus, love will make you share in His virtues and give you the strength to practice them in spite of all obstacles. To know and love Jesus Christ is your highest gain both for time and eternity. No sacrifice can be too great to attain it. You have true wisdom, holiness, and happiness insofar as you know and love Jesus Christ.

∞

Make atonement through the Eucharist

The second essential act of devotion to the Sacred Heart is atonement. The love of Jesus is dishonored by the ingratitude of men, as He Himself declared in the third great apparition to St. Margaret Mary: "Behold this Heart which has so loved men that it has spared nothing, even to exhausting and consuming itself, in order to testify its love. In return, I receive from the greater part only ingratitude, by their irreverence and sacrileges, and by the coldness and contempt they have for me in this Sacrament of Love."

Then He asked her to atone for these ingratitudes by the ardor of her own love: "My daughter, I come into the heart I have given you in order that through your fervor you may atone for the offenses which I have received from lukewarm and slothful hearts which dishonor me in the Blessed Sacrament."

Your devotion to the Sacred Heart should be an act of reparation and atonement for your own ingratitude and the ingratitude of all men for the love He has for us, above all in the Blessed Sacrament.

Receive Holy Communion often, especially on the first Fridays of nine consecutive months; spend some time before the Blessed Sacrament; perform little penances to prove by your actions that you want to make reparation. Make a holy hour some day or evening before the Sacred Heart in the tabernacle. Your love will be reparation for all human forgetfulness of His love. The Sacred Heart will never be outdone in love and generosity to you.

Frequent Holy Communion — together with the Mass — is by far the easiest and most perfect form of reparation you can offer to God. When you receive Holy Communion, you make an act of faith, for your presence at the Lord's Table is proof of your belief that Jesus is truly present in the Blessed Sacrament. You make an act of hope, because you believe in our Lord's promises and hope for the graces attached to receiving Holy Communion. You make an act of love, for by receiving Holy Communion, you are pleasing Jesus, who has instituted this great Sacrament of Love for us. You make an act of humility, for you acknowledge your need of and dependence on God and the spiritual strength received through the Eucharist. You offer to God a pure and holy sacrifice most pleasing to His divine majesty.

Holy Mass and Communion are the greatest spiritual weapons God has placed at our disposal to help bring about peace. They are far more powerful than all atom and hydrogen bombs, guided missiles, guns, planes, tanks, and ships combined. Many times during his pontificate, Pope Pius XII urged frequent reception of Holy Communion, stating, "Men will always find the best remedy against serious evils in the Eucharist. . . . Only through frequent reception of our Divine Lord will they have the strength to help a world darkened by ignorance and gripped in the ice of indifference."

Our Lady of Fatima appealed for frequent Communion as a counteroffensive against Communism and the forces of evil. At Fatima, Portugal, in 1917, the need was clearly stated for making reparation to Almighty God, in order to appease His just wrath, aroused by the many horrible sins and sacrileges committed against Him. On one occasion, the guardian angel of Portugal appeared to the three children, bearing a golden chalice in one hand and a Host in the other. The amazed children noticed that drops of blood were falling from the Host into the chalice. Then the angel left both suspended in midair and prostrated himself on the ground, saying this beautiful prayer: "Most Holy Trinity — Father, Son, and Holy Spirit — I adore You profoundly. I offer You the most precious Body, Blood, Soul, and divinity of Jesus Christ, present in all the tabernacles of the world, in reparation for the outrages, sacrileges, and indifferences whereby He is offended. Through the infinite merits of His Most Sacred Heart and the Immaculate Heart of Mary, I beg of You the conversion of poor sinners."

If we could get even a majority of Catholic men, women, and children to offer each reception of the Eucharist in reparation for the sins of the world, in reparation for their own sins, and for the conversion of the world, we would help offset to a great extent the hatred of enemies who are trying to destroy God's Church. For the sake of this love, God would shower mercy on them instead of justice, and would pour graces into their hearts to see the error of their ways.

This act of atonement is highly sanctifying. Atonement will further enkindle your fervor by enabling you to sympathize with the sufferings of Jesus. It will help you to endure all the trials that God may send you; for love of Him and in union with His sufferings, it will bring peace to the world. Thus, devotion to the Sacred Heart demands a blending of love and sacrifice, and this is the very spirit of Christianity.

∞

Find graces through Holy Hours

Eucharistic life is indispensable in the life of a good Catholic. The many graces and blessings received through holy Mass and Communion, and through frequent visits to the Blessed Sacrament, are the surest guarantee of peace and happiness in your life. It is through the Eucharist that Jesus reaches your soul, even more effectively than He did in the days of His earthly sojourn among men. The Holy Hour is a very powerful means of developing eucharistic life.

St. Margaret Mary Alacoque was to be the means of spreading devotion to the Sacred Heart and the Holy Hour. While she was rapt in prayer before the altar, in the year 1675, our Lord appeared to this Visitation nun and showed Himself in glory with His five wounds shining like five brilliant suns and His Sacred Heart as a furnace of fire. He said, "Behold this Heart that has loved men so much that it has spared nothing to testify to them its love; and in return I receive from most of them only ingratitude by their irreverences and their sacrileges and by the coldness and contempt they have for me in the Sacrament of Love." One of the devotions our Lord taught her was that of the Holy Hour.

Our Savior, in His agony in the garden went to His apostles Peter, James, and John to seek a little consolation from them, but He found them asleep. He said to them, "So, could you not watch with me one hour? Watch and pray that you may not enter into temptation."[66] Jesus asked St. Margaret Mary to honor His Sacred Heart by rising every Thursday night at eleven o'clock and prostrating herself for an hour before Him in the Blessed Sacrament. During the hour, she was to implore God's mercy for poor sinners and to sweeten the bitterness He felt when His apostles slept during His agony in the Garden of Olives.

Many priests will tell you that they owe their vocation to a saintly mother's prayers. There can be little doubt that Herbert Cardinal Vaughan, once Archbishop of Westminster, England, owed his vocation to the priesthood to his mother's prayers before the Blessed Sacrament. For nearly twenty years, it was Mrs. Vaughan's daily practice to spend an hour in prayer before the Blessed Sacrament, asking that her sons might become priests. In answer to her prayers, six of her eight sons became priests. Of the six priests, three became bishops and one a cardinal. Her five daughters eventually entered convents.

Who can tell how great an influence the good example of parents will have on their children if they are willing to dedicate some of their time to our Lord in the Blessed Sacrament? Actions speak louder than words. The good results such parents will obtain

---

[66] Matt. 26:40-41.

in the duties assigned to them in the family will correspond invariably to the degree of eucharistic life they acquire. The important lesson their children will learn is that their family needs Jesus in the Blessed Sacrament. Their mother and father go to Him to beg for His help; nothing could be a better incentive for children to do the same.

There is no way to describe the tremendous effects that praying mothers and fathers have on their families. The Eucharist is the powerhouse of grace and a treasury of blessing, but we must make contact with the Eucharist. Young people, brothers and sisters in the family, can gain the strength they need to keep their souls sinless in the midst of the spirit of the world in which they live, if only they will spend more time with Him who loved children so fondly and graciously blessed them during His earthly life, and who today in the tabernacle is the Friend of youth. The virtue that friendship with Jesus will impart will be a source of the greatest joy to devoted parents and a means of blessing for their families.

If you are in earnest about helping your own soul and the souls of those who belong to your family, resolve to visit your eucharistic Savior whenever possible. If you are in earnest about reestablishing your own family in Christ, you will find some time during the week for a visit to the Blessed Sacrament or a Holy Hour. Even though you are very busy, you can always find time for prayer if you really want to. Your visit may also include your Rosary, the Way of the Cross, or spiritual reading. This can be done by attending a devotion and Benediction in your parish church, or by arriving half an hour early for your weekday Mass or staying half an hour after Mass, or by making a special visit to the church on a Sunday afternoon or on the First Friday of the month. Such a practice would be a source of great blessing for you and for souls. It would permit the influence of Jesus to exert itself in your home, and His peace and joy to fill the hearts of those you love.

Part Two

✤

The Holy Sacrifice
of the Mass

Chapter Five

∞

Understand the Sacrifice of the Cross

To understand the Mass, we must first understand what a sacrifice is. It is the offering of a victim by a priest to God alone, and the destruction of it in some way to acknowledge that He is the Creator and Lord of all things. The word *sacrifice* means "something made sacred." It is a gift that a priest offers to God as a sign that those offering belong entirely to Him. The gift is destroyed to show God that the people offering the sacrifice wish to belong to Him alone and that they want to make up for the wrong they have done Him. Therefore, sacrifice expresses obedience and atonement.

A sacrifice requires an altar, a visible gift or victim, and a priest. It must be offered to God alone and must be an outward sacrificial offering — by which it is consecrated to God — as well as an inward offering of the heart — to acknowledge that God is the Creator and Lord of all.

A group of persons may pray by sign, offering a gift to God in token of their inward dispositions. They do this through someone elected or appointed to act in their name — that is, through a priest. When the priest makes the offering in the name of the people, he puts the visible gift on the altar with a certain ceremony or holy action. In this way, the gift passes at once from the ownership of the people into the possession of God and thereby becomes sacred or consecrated. In other words, it is offered as a *sacrifice* to the Lord. A sacrifice is more than public prayer; it is a public action, the greatest act of public worship. By it we acknowledge that God is the Creator and Lord of all and that we depend entirely upon Him.

The outward offering of the gift signifies the inward offering or consecration of our life to God. From the earliest times, men have offered God two kinds of gifts. They were either unbloody gifts, such as corn, oil, bread, or the firstfruits of the fields; or bloody gifts, such as sheep, lambs, calves, or heifers. These gifts signified human life, and by publicly offering such gifts, the people wished to express by sign that they consecrated, or gave back to God, their own life, which they had received from Him.

The first children of Adam and Eve were Cain and Abel. Cain grew up to be a farmer, and Abel became a shepherd. Cain and Abel offered gifts to God as a sacrifice. Cain offered fruit and grain; Abel offered a lamb of his flock. They offered these gifts to God by burning them. This expressed that they depended on God for everything as their Creator and that they were willing to obey Him in all His laws. Since Abel could not take his own life to show that He depended upon God, he offered the life of a lamb, which took his place. All this was a sign that Abel wanted to give himself and all he had to God, and that he wanted to be obedient.

When God saw that Cain's heart was full of evil, He was not pleased with his gifts. But God was pleased with Abel's gifts because his heart was full of goodness, and he offered his gifts to God with a better spirit.

Sacrifice expresses atonement for sin. By sin man offended God and deserved the penalty of death. By killing an animal and offering it to God, man wanted to show that he was willing to devote his life to God in obedient service in atonement for his sins.

In the ceremonies of the annual day of atonement in the Old Testament, the high priest laid his hands upon the head of a scapegoat as a sign that he was putting upon this animal all the sins of the people who stood around him. Then the scapegoat was led forth and driven into the desert, where it perished. This was a sign that the people's sins were destroyed with the life of the animal.[67]

After the Deluge, Noah built an altar and offered to God a sacrifice of thanksgiving. Melchizedek, the king of Salem and a priest of the Most High God, offered a sacrifice of bread and wine.[68] Abraham was ready to offer his only son in sacrifice.[69] Moses, too, built an altar at the foot of the mountain and offered sacrifices to the Lord.[70] At the dedication of the Temple, King Solomon offered a great number of victims in sacrifice.[71] The prophet Elijah prayed to God to accept his sacrifice.[72] In obedience to the Lord's command, the Israelites each offered two lambs in sacrifice at the Temple of Jerusalem, one in the morning and another in the evening.[73]

∞

Christ's Sacrifice of the Cross redeemed you

These sacrifices of animals, offered by the Jews and even by pagans, could not of themselves take away sin, but they did express how earnestly man longed for a real redemption. After Adam's Fall, the souls of all men were soiled by Original Sin. Someone had to come from Heaven to redeem the world.

Through God's infinite mercy, this redemption was brought about when Jesus Christ, the Son of God, became man and offered

[67] Cf. Lev. 16:20-22.
[68] Gen. 14:18.
[69] Gen. 22:1 ff.
[70] Exod. 24:4.
[71] 2 Chron. 7:5.
[72] 1 Kings 18:36-38.
[73] Exod. 29:38-39.

Himself as a sacrifice to take away the sins of the world. Jesus could represent us, because He was man. As man, He could die in atonement for sin, and, as God, He could offer a sacrifice of limitless value. Our sins against God demanded an atonement that only God could make because the offense was infinite. These sufferings and death of the God-Man on the Cross are the one perfect sacrifice that takes away the sins of the world.

St. Leo I[74] wrote, "He is our true and eternal High Priest, whose governance can have neither change nor end, He whose type was shown by the priest Melchizedek, not offering Jewish victims to God, but offering the sacrifice of that mystery, which our Redeemer consecrated in His own Body and Blood."

The Sacrifice of the New Testament is Jesus Christ Himself, who by His death on the Cross offered Himself to His heavenly Father for us. The six points required for a sacrifice are found in the sacrifice of Jesus on the Cross. The altar was the Cross. The sacrificial gift was the Body and Blood of Christ, the Lamb of God Himself. The priest was Christ Himself, the High Priest who stood as Mediator before God on behalf of sinful mankind. He offered Himself in sacrifice to the offended God, the Most Holy Trinity, out of love and pity for us.

The outward offering was made when, as Redeemer, Jesus freely offered His Blood for mankind as a sacrifice, while submitting to the forcible shedding of His Blood by His executioners. His tormentors were the instruments; Christ was the High Priest, and God was pleased only in what His Son did. The inward offering that Jesus made to God on the Cross was His Sacred Heart. By sin, men had dishonored God.

By His sacrifice on the Cross, Jesus gave back to God once more the honor that is due to Him. Jesus appeased God's just anger, reconciled us sinners with God, and so redeemed us. By His

[74] St. Leo I (d. 461), Pope from 440.

Sacrifice on the Cross, Jesus adored God as His Lord and gave Him honor and praise in the fullest measure.

Pope Pius XII says, "To the unbloody gift of Himself, under the appearance of bread and wine, Our Savior, Jesus Christ, wished, as a special proof of His intimate and infinite love to add the bloody Sacrifice of the Cross. Indeed, in His way of acting, He gave an example of that sublime charity which He set before His disciples as the highest measure of love: 'Greater love than this no one has, that one lay down his life for his friends' (John 15:13). Wherefore, the love of Jesus Christ, the Son of God, by the Sacrifice of Golgotha, clearly and richly proves the love of God Himself: 'In this we have come to know His love, that He laid down His life for us; and we likewise ought to lay down our life for the brethren' (John 2:16). And in fact Our Divine Redeemer was nailed to the Cross more by His love than by the force of the executioners. His voluntary holocaust is the supreme gift which He bestowed on each man according to the concise words of the Apostle: 'Who loved me, and gave Himself up for me' (Gal. 2:20)."[75]

[75] *Haurietis Aquas*, sect. 73-74.

Chapter Six

∞

Remember Christ's sacrificial death in the Mass

All sacrifice did not cease with the death of Jesus on the Cross. He left us the Holy Eucharist as a visible sacrifice, in order to represent continually that which was once accomplished on the Cross, and to apply the fruits of it to our souls. Jesus willed to make His Sacrifice on the Cross ever present in His Church, so He instituted the Sacrifice of the Mass at the Last Supper when He offered His Body and Blood for the first time under the appearances of bread and wine. The next day, on Good Friday, Jesus offered Himself in a bloody manner on the Cross.

We could not go to Calvary to offer ourselves with Him and thus share in the fruits of His Sacrifice; so Jesus brought Calvary to us. With the thought of Calvary uppermost in His mind, the Savior said to His Apostles, "Take and eat; for this is my Body, which is being given for you. All of you, drink of this; for this is my Blood of the new covenant, which is being shed for many unto the forgiveness of sins. Do this in remembrance of me." Jesus gave us His own Body and Blood in the Holy Eucharist and commanded His Apostles to do as He had just done. Thus through the Mass He continues and renews His Sacrifice on the Cross. All who participate in holy Mass, especially by receiving His sacrificial Body and

Blood in Holy Communion, become one sacrifice with Him, thus sharing in the heavenly fruits or merits obtained by His death on the Cross.

In the declarations of the Council of Trent is this: "Jesus Christ, our God and our Savior, although He was to offer Himself once and for all to God the Father on the altar of the Cross by His death, there to work out our eternal redemption, yet since His priesthood was not to be extinguished by His death, He, at the Last Supper, on the night on which He was betrayed, in order to leave to His beloved spouse, the Church, a visible Sacrifice such as the exigencies of our nature demanded, wherein that sacrifice of blood once and for all to be wrought upon the Cross should be represented and its memory abide to the end of the world . . . offered His Body and Blood to God the Father under the appearance of bread and wine, and gave it under the same appearances to His Apostles, whom He then appointed priests of the New Testament; to them, too, and to their successors in the priesthood. He, by the words: 'Do this in remembrance of me,' gave the command to offer it, as the Catholic Church has always understood and taught."

∞

The Mass is a living memorial of Jesus' Passion

The Mass presents to the faithful, in the form of sign and symbol, the death on the Cross. Christ died on the Cross by shedding all His Precious Blood on our behalf. St. Paul stresses this point of the Blood being poured forth and thus completely separated from the Body. On the altar there is enacted a sacramental or symbolic separation of Body and Blood. It is a sacramental re-presentation of the real separation that took place on Calvary. It shows forth the death on the Cross. Hence the Church sings, "O Sacred Banquet, in which Christ is received, the memory of His Passion is renewed, the mind is filled with grace, and a pledge of future glory is given to us."

Remember Christ's sacrificial death in the Mass

At Mass we remember Jesus, especially His great love for us which He proved by His Passion and death. We fulfill His last will, because bread and wine are changed into His Body and Blood. The living presence of the Savior who died for us is still truly with us, for He said at the Last Supper, "This is my Body which is given for you; this is my Blood of the new covenant, which is being shed for you."[76]

His painful death on the Cross is represented at Mass by the double consecration of the bread and wine. The Sacred Host separated from the chalice reminds us of the slow bleeding by which His Blood was separated from His Body on the Cross.

The Sacrifice of Jesus, the Head of mankind, has been the great sacrifice of the world. It has been an eloquent declaration, made in the name of the whole human race, that it repents for sins and rejects sin and that it wishes to be consecrated to the glory of God. It has been the one, true, perfect Sacrifice, in itself and of itself acceptable to God.

The mission of the Church is to render God worship worthy of Him, and it does so through sacrifice. The Sacrifice of Jesus on the Cross is perpetuated; it is continually being offered in the Church and shall be until the end of time. Calvary is re-presented — continually presented to our senses — in the Mass. The Mass is a living memorial of our Lord.

Over every Catholic altar there is a crucifix to remind us that the Mass is the same sacrifice as the Sacrifice of the Cross, because in the Mass the victim and the principal priest is Jesus Christ. The crucifix speaks silently: "He died for us." The Mass is a monument or memorial of His death by which He saved our souls.

[76] Cf. 1 Cor. 11:24-25.

Chapter Seven

∞

Participate in the Sacrifice of the Mass

The rite enacted on the altar is not only a sign or memorial of what took place on Good Friday. It is also a true sacrifice — a mystical immolation of Christ enacted here and now before the eyes of the faithful. This is the real Body and Blood of Jesus Christ. He is present under the sacramental covering — the appearances of bread and wine — and appears in the form of a victim through the sacramental separation of Blood from Body that takes place in our presence.

∞

The Sacrifice of the Cross differs
from the Sacrifice of the Mass

The Sacrifice of the Cross and the Sacrifice of the Mass differ. The manner in which the Sacrifice is offered is different: on the Cross, Christ physically shed His Blood and was physically slain; in the Mass, there is no physical shedding of Blood nor physical death, because Christ can die no more. In the Holy Eucharist on our altars, our Savior Jesus Christ, Body and Blood, Soul and divinity, is really present under the appearances of bread and wine. He is present there, not in the manner of a material body, but in the manner of a spirit. His was a spiritual Body after the Resurrection.

In the Holy Eucharist the glorified Body of Jesus can no longer be physically injured or deprived of life. It is not necessary that Christ should actually suffer and die again in holy Mass. He did that "once for all"[77] on Calvary. In the Mass there is no physical shedding of blood or physical death. Jesus offers Himself in the Mass as an unbloody Sacrifice.

When Jesus instituted the Holy Eucharist, He willed once for all to be present as a sacrificial victim: "This is my Body, which is being given for you. This is my Blood of the new covenant, which is being shed for many unto the forgiveness of sins." Each time the Holy Eucharist is celebrated, Jesus is present with the intention of offering Himself in sacrifice. By the words of consecration, He becomes present under the forms of bread and wine, the unbloody symbols of His bloody death on the Cross. He intends thereby to remind the faithful of His Sacrifice on Calvary. At the same time, He also wills to present Himself, as Priest and Victim, to God for them, in order to enable them to offer a visible sacrifice together with Him.

After the Consecration, Jesus becomes present on the altar as the Priest and Victim of Calvary, and, through the hands of the priest, He offers Himself again to His Father with all the acts of adoration, abandonment, and love He once offered to Him on the Cross. The altar is another Calvary; for that which is offered and given upon the altar is the Body that suffered for us and the Blood that was shed for our salvation. The Last Supper, the Sacrifice of the Cross, and holy Mass are one and the same sacrifice, and Jesus is the only Victim.

On the Cross Christ gained merit and satisfied for us, while in the Mass He applies to us the merits and satisfaction of His death on the Cross. On the Cross Christ freely accepted His sufferings and death. He offered His life in the most perfect and loving

[77] Rom. 6:10.

obedience to the Father and in heroic love for men. By this means He, in our stead, fully appeased God's just anger at our sins and reconciled the world and its Creator. At the same time He earned for us an inexhaustible treasury of grace that enables us to regain the right to be children of God and heirs to Heaven. In the Mass He offers Himself with the same loving obedience to the will of God as on the Cross. But now He offers to God the fruits of His Sacrifice on the Cross, ever renewing His petition to God to apply the saving effects of His bloody sacrifice to us.

The Last Supper, the Sacrifice of the Cross, and holy Mass are one and the same Sacrifice, and Jesus is the only Victim. At the Last Supper He made one offering of Himself to His heavenly Father. It was carried out and completed on the Cross and is continued throughout all time by His priests at holy Mass. On Calvary He redeemed us and merited graces for us. Our souls receive these graces at holy Mass.

By virtue of the Holy Sacrifice of the Mass, you are infinitely rich. A single holy Mass is in value equal to the Sacrifice of Christ on the Cross. The saints and all pious Christians have treasured holy Mass highly. Some saints used to visit their church half an hour before holy Mass and prepare themselves for this touching drama by gazing and meditating upon the crucified Savior. Looking at a crucifix is a very good preparation for holy Mass. There you see best of all Christ's love for you. That love sacrificed itself for you on the Cross, and each day it continues that Sacrifice on the altar at holy Mass.

∞

The entire Church offers Christ in the Mass

At the altar Christ stands with the Body that has been sacrificed on Calvary. At Mass the Mystical Body, united with Christ, offers with Him, the Victim on the altar, and is co-offered with Him. The faithful offer, not as true priests, but as being legitimately represented by their High Priest and His visible priest, who offer the sacrifice in the name of the whole Church.

Jesus Christ, the Son of Man, is always the principal and sovereign Priest. From Him the Apostles and their successors in the priesthood received the power to offer the eucharistic Sacrifice in His name and on behalf of the whole Church. He imparts some elements of His priestly character to the faithful also, for He raises all those who have received the baptismal mark to the dignity of being instruments of His priesthood, in virtue of which the Church offers herself in union with Christ. Since the external rite is always a sign of interior sacrifice, the Mystical Body, through and in Jesus, offers the real Body and Blood of Christ, present under the appearances of bread and wine, as a pledge of its own oblation and devotion to God. In the Mass, the living members of Christ unite themselves with His Sacrifice by taking their part in the expiation and adoration offered by their Head, Jesus Christ. In Christ's submission to God, they submit to God.

St. Thomas Aquinas says, "There is one Christ, not many offered by Christ and by us. For Christ was offered once, and His sacrifice was the original of ours. There is one Body, not many, and so, wherever He is offered, the sacrifice is one and the same with His."

In the encyclical letter of Pope Pius XII on the Mystical Body of Christ, we read, "By means of the eucharistic Sacrifice Christ our Lord willed to give to the faithful a striking manifestation of our union among ourselves and with our divine Head, wonderful as it is and beyond all praise. For in this Sacrifice the sacred minister acts as the vicegerent not only of our Savior but of the whole Mystical Body and of each one of the faithful. In this act of Sacrifice through the hands of the priest, by whose word alone the Immaculate Lamb is present on the altar, the faithful themselves, united with him in prayer and desire, offer to the Eternal Father a most acceptable Victim of praise and propitiation for the needs of the whole Church. And as the Divine Redeemer, when dying on the

Cross, offered Himself to the Eternal Father, as Head of the whole human race, so 'in this clean oblation' (Mal. 1:11) He offers to the heavenly Father not only Himself as Head of the Church, but in Himself His mystical members also, since He holds them all, even those who are weak and ailing, in His most loving Heart."[78]

Thus, the Sacrifice of the Mass is not the act of an individual Christian: it is a public and social act and is of the whole Church — Head and members. The surrender of self is always real and perfect on the part of Jesus, the Supreme Priest and Victim. It is very real also on the part of those who are in the state of grace and are actually united with Him by charity. Hence, the Mass is always agreeable to God. It is infinitely agreeable as regards the Victim, Jesus; it is more or less agreeable as regards the individual Christian, and in the measure in which he really possesses the disposition of heart — absolute submission to the will of God — that is found in the Heart of Jesus. Sin and attachment to sin are the obstacles to sanctity. At Mass the member of Christ professes to endeavor to overcome these obstacles.

The interior immolation, then, of the Holy Sacrifice of the Altar is that of Christ Himself and all the members of the Mystical Body in union with Him. The members of Christ have a very active part to take in the Sacrifice of the Mass. It is their duty to unite themselves in the sacramental oblation of their Head and to offer themselves in union with Him.

At His death on Calvary, Jesus gave back to His Father His bodily members, nailed to a Cross and covered with Blood, as a visible expression of His Sacrifice for our sins. Christ gives us His own Body and Blood in the Holy Eucharist, to be offered as a sacrifice commemorating and renewing for all time the Sacrifice of the Cross. In Holy Communion He draws to Himself and into Himself the members of His Mystical Body, the Church, in order that He

---

[78] *Mystici Corporis* (June 29, 1943), sect. 82.

may give them as a sacrificial gift to the Father. Thus, by the great power of His love, He wishes to join us in a living union with His Mystical Body, as one sacrifice, so that that Body may grow until God comes to judge the world.

Offer yourself together with Christ to the Father in deepest humility and with sincerest love. Recall that when you receive Holy Communion, you are partaking of the sacrificial Body and Blood of the Lord, thus becoming one sacrifice with Him for the glory of God and your own sanctification.

∞

In the Mass, you are a co-victim with Christ

Faith tells you that during the Mass Jesus offers Himself to His Father just as He did on the Cross — although in an unbloody manner — and in the same spirit of love and resignation to His Divine Will, because He is present in the Sacred Host as the Victim of Calvary. But it is then only that He is really your Victim when you offer yourself with Him on the altar in order to share by your generosity in His life of self-sacrifice. You are a member of the Church, His Mystical Body, and consequently you cannot remain inactive when, as the Head of the Body, Jesus is sacrificing Himself.

For this reason you should unite all the work, pains, and disappointments of your life with His sacrifice at holy Mass, in that spirit of loving resignation and devoted obedience in which He makes His offering. You will then gladly accept all that God may see fit to send you — the pleasant and the unpleasant, joy and sorrow. What a marvelous effect this will have on your life! In this way the works and sufferings of your life will become most precious in God's sight — even though they are poor in themselves — because they are one with the divine Sacrifice of Jesus at Mass. All the acts of the eternal High Priest, by which He renews upon the altar His Sacrifice of Calvary, become yours.

Pope Pius XI, in his encyclical on reparation, writes, "Because of the wonderful dispensation of Divine Wisdom, by which what is lacking of the sufferings of Christ for His Body, which is the Church, is to be filled up in our flesh, we can add, nay, even we are bound to add, our own praises and satisfactions to the praises and satisfaction 'which Christ rendered unto God in the name of sinners.' But we must always remember that the whole virtue of the expiation depends on the one sacrifice of Christ in blood, which is renewed without intermission on our altars in a bloodless manner, for the Victim is one and the same; He who then offered Himself on the Cross is now offering through the ministry of the priests, the manner of offering only being different. Therefore with the Most August Sacrifice of the Eucharist an oblation of the ministers and the other faithful should be joined, that they also may present themselves living victims, holy, pleasing to God. . . . The more perfectly our oblation and sacrifice correspond with the Lord's sacrifice, that is to say, the more perfectly we immolate our self-love and our desires, and crucify our flesh with that mystic crucifixion of which the Apostle speaks, the more abundant fruits of that propitiation and expiation shall we reap for ourselves and others."

The sacrifice in each Mass is Jesus in His entirety — Jesus, the priest, and the people. The priest says, "Pray, that our sacrifice . . ." This is your Mass, too. Do not just attend, but take an active part in it. The Church expects your interior offering. At the Roman Council of 1076, Pope Gregory VII made it the duty of every Christian to offer something to God during holy Mass.

What we have to offer is very small, yet, when united with the Sacrifice of Christ at holy Mass, that offering becomes beautiful and precious. But the interior offering requires that we give all.

In the book of Revelation, St. John describes Heaven. On the altar, the Lamb lies alive, but as if slain. Around Him are twenty-four ancients clothed in white robes and crowned with gold and thousands of angels hymning the sacrifice and triumph of the Lamb.[79] This magnificent scene takes place on earth at each Mass if each Christian shares in the Sacrifice.

Strive to cleanse your soul from all mortal sin in order to be fit to partake of the Victim. Have a hatred of all deliberate venial sins. The measure of profit you draw from the Mass is the measure in which you offer yourself in union with Christ.

∞

Your daily life should reflect the Mass

By taking part in the Holy Sacrifice of the Altar, you profess to accept as your own the sacrificial dispositions of Jesus. You must therefore live a life of sacrifice, a life of Christlike obedience to God.

The reason we have so little spirit of sacrifice, in spite of the many Masses offered and so many Communions received, is that we do not have the right spirit at the Holy Sacrifice. If you truly pray the Mass with true understanding of your own part as victim, you will surely come to live your Mass and to fit into your day's work the spirit of sacrifice it demands.

How are you to live the Mass in your daily life? For our Lord, the Eucharist is the sacrament of self-immolation, and the sacrament in which He gives His entire self.

You may emphasize the aspect of submission or that of sacrifice. Some desire to imitate the sovereign activity of our Lord offering Himself. They cannot be content with accepting all that God is pleased to send them, but they seek opportunities to make sacrifices.

A host is made of small grains, each one of them insignificant. As many as necessary are used and then exposed to the heat of a gentle fire. Your intention of being united to Jesus the Victim

[79] Rev. 4:4; 5:6, 11-12.

stamps these ground grains with the mark of the Cross. You should be a true sharer of the Sacrifice; at the side of the immolated Savior should be your own immolation, which Jesus expects.

You should receive Communion in the spirit of a victim — that is, with the intention of giving our Lord this addition to His Sacrifice, which He needs so that His Father may be fully glorified and so that more souls may be saved. To receive Communion is not only to *receive*, for it is a Treasure, but also to *give*, and to give something that will make of you and of the Victim one gift. You cannot be one with the Victim without yourself being a victim. Your motto should be: "I live for Jesus Christ, and Jesus Christ lives in me."

A Communion well made presupposes union — Jesus and he who receives Him truly become one!

How far removed from this understanding of the Mass is the sharing in the Mass that does not affect in any way whatever the daily conduct of the Christian! But understood as it should be, the Mass becomes a vital religious act, the center from which all other activity radiates. At the Mass, associating yourself with the Victim, you give yourself, in union with Him, without reserve to regulating your life according to the divine will. Your life after Mass ought to be the practical carrying out of the submission to God you have promised at the immolation of the Victim of the Mass. Your acts of the day ought to prove the sincerity of your daily sacrifice. Thus you will keep your body pure, and you will make of it an instrument for the glory of God — a living victim, holy and agreeable to God.

Chapter Eight

Receive the benefits of the Mass

Adoration: The first purpose for which the Mass is offered is to adore God as our Creator and Lord.

You may ask yourself, "How can I honor and glorify God in the best possible way?" When you make the Stations of the Cross or recite the Rosary, you give honor to God. When you are kind, He is pleased with your deed of charity. But none of these things has the same value as a single holy Mass.

Were you by yourself alone to honor and adore God, you would be doing little indeed. And even if all the angels and saints joined with you in adoring God, that also would not be worthy of God. The reason holy Mass is such a glorious and sublime sacrifice of adoration and praise is that Jesus Himself is present on the altar in holy Mass. He unites our adoration and praise with His.

In his twenty-fifth year, St. Thomas More, the Chancellor of England, had serious thoughts of becoming a religious. "The world was made up," he wrote, "of false love and flattery, of hatred and quarrels, and of all that ministered to the body and the Devil." Being near the Carthusians, he imitated their penances, said the Divine Office and the Penitential Psalms, and heard Mass daily. This practice he continued throughout his life and observed it so religiously that when King Henry VIII once sent for him while he was hearing Mass, he would not stir until the Mass was finished, even though he was told the message was urgent. The saint sent this message to the king: "As soon as my audience with the King of Heaven is ended, I will at once obey the desire of my earthly king."

Thomas More realized that his first duty was to adore God, his Creator, and that this adoration was paid in an infinite degree by Jesus Christ in the Mass. The humble and obedient Sacrifice of the Savior offered on the Cross, and renewed on the altar, gave infinite adoration to God, because Jesus was the Son of God.

Thanksgiving: The second purpose for which the Mass is offered is to thank God for His many favors.

How often God has secretly admonished you to do good, warned you against evil, and preserved you from the dangers of sin! How many graces you have received through the sacraments and in answer to your prayers! How many natural gifts you also owe to God! The best way to show your gratitude to God for all He has given you is to join with the priest in offering holy Mass, where Jesus Himself thanks God for you and with you and offers Himself as a sacrificial gift of thanksgiving.

Make it a point to express your gratitude to God for the many things for which you owe Him thanks by having holy Mass offered in thanksgiving. After recovering from a serious illness, or after the successful accomplishment of some important undertaking, have a Mass offered in appreciation. Recall anniversaries by assisting at a Mass of thanksgiving. Join with the priest in offering thanks to God for all past favors. The best way to obtain further favors is to be grateful for past blessings.

You can also honor the memory of the saints in Mass by thanking God for the grace and glory bestowed upon them and by asking their intercession. The sacrifice of the Mass belongs to God alone. But in the Mass you also greet God's friends, the saints of Heaven. This is pleasing to God. By honoring them, we give honor to God, who made them what they are.

Petition: The third purpose for which the Mass is offered is to ask God to bestow His blessings on you and all men.

Many evils of soul and body threaten you. You may be exposed to sickness or an accident that might end in death. Temptations may assail you, and you may even fall into serious sin. To obtain the blessings you need, offer holy Mass.

If there is sickness in your family, if you are in need of special help, attend holy Mass and beg God for the help you need, especially for the grace of a happy death. Jesus Himself is your Mediator before God's throne in Heaven and pleads for you in the Mass. You do not pray alone; Christ prays with you and for you. He shows the marks of His sacred wounds to the Father, and pleads for you.

Reparation: The fourth purpose for which the Mass is offered is to satisfy the justice of God for the sins committed against Him.

Most Christians depart from this life with the burden of venial sins and the unpaid debt of temporal punishment for sin. They must suffer as poor souls in Purgatory until God's justice has been satisfied. We can shorten their Purgatory by having Mass offered in their behalf.

Every Mass is a sacrifice of propitiation not only for the dead but also for sinners still living on earth. When you pray, fast, give alms, or perform little acts of self-denial, you make satisfaction for your sins. But all that is as nothing in comparison with the power of a single holy Mass, for on the altar Christ satisfies and appeases God for you and with you.

The eucharistic sacrifice does not directly and immediately cancel mortal sins, but it does contribute indirectly to their forgiveness. For holy Mass calms the righteous anger of God and induces Him to regard the sinner with favor and mercy and to remit in whole or in part the punishment due to sin. Appeased by the offering of His Son in holy Mass, God is disposed to grant the grace of penitence and sincere conversion, so that the sinner may properly receive the sacrament of Penance for the forgiveness of his sins.

Venial sins, too, are thus forgiven indirectly through the sacrifice of propitiation. God gives us the grace we need so that we may truly repent. But if we are properly disposed, the temporal punishments due to sins (which remain after the sins have been forgiven) are directly canceled, at least in part through holy Mass. Thus holy Mass can shorten the time of your punishment in Purgatory.

The Mass is so powerful because at the consecration the priest lifts up God's own dear Son, as if to say, "O God, for the sake of Your Son have mercy on us." And Jesus Himself calls out as He once did on the Cross, "Father, forgive them."[80] God cannot refuse that prayer.

∞

The Mass offers many fruits

The value or fruit of the Mass is infinite if we consider the gift offered but finite if we consider the offering of the gift. The measure of the fruits of the Mass depends chiefly on the dispositions, that is, the degree of holiness of those who offer it — the Church, the priest, and the faithful.

The fruits of the Mass are applied in general to the whole Church, both to the living and the dead. The celebrant includes all the children of the Church in the Holy Sacrifice. In fact, the whole world feels the effects of the fruits of the Mass.

The fruits of the Mass are applied first, in particular, to the priest who celebrates the Mass; then to those for whom the priest especially offers it; and finally to all those who assist at it with devotion. Of course, the best method of assisting at Mass is to unite with the priest in offering the Holy Sacrifice and to receive Holy Communion. The fruits of the Mass depend in great measure on

[80] Luke 23:34.

the devotion of the participants. Since you are offering the Holy Sacrifice with the priest, you should be filled with a true spirit of sacrifice by uniting your works, joys, and sufferings of each day in union with Jesus, the Victim on the altar. In order that the fruits of holy Mass may reach your soul more surely and more effectively, receive Holy Communion at every Mass.

The fruits or graces of holy Mass are manifold. Each person receives what he needs. The sinner obtains grace to repent and amend his life; a person in the state of sanctifying grace receives further grace to enable him to become more holy. One who is exposed to temptations receives strength and courage to resist valiantly; one who is sad and discouraged obtains comfort and consolation; one who is in need obtains the necessary aid. The dying get special help for their last struggle; the poor souls are comforted in their sufferings or redeemed entirely from Purgatory.

∞

Go to Mass daily

Daily Mass holds the same spiritual treasure as the Mass you attend on Sunday. You can gain great graces here below and lay up for yourself treasure in Heaven by attending Mass daily instead of just once a week.

Just one Mass gives God more praise and thanksgiving than the combined worship of all the angels and saints. Just one Mass has greater power of atoning for sin than all the sacrifice of all the faithful on earth. Just one Mass can do more for the souls in Purgatory than all our prayers for them and all their own sufferings. Jesus makes the infinite riches of His Holy Sacrifice available to us each time one of His priests offers holy Mass.

Hearing Mass daily can help you and your family to avoid temptation and sin, to find peace amid the trials of life, to grow in the love of God, to thank God for all His blessings, to obtain protection against all dangers, to gain the favors of which you stand in need, and to shorten the Purgatory of your dear departed ones, as well as your own. St. John Fisher once wrote, "The Mass is like the sun which daily illumines and warms all Christian life."

You cannot afford to miss using this greatest treasure of the Church. Make it your greatest treasure, too, by going to Mass daily!

Part Three

∞

Holy Communion

.

Chapter Nine

∞

Nourish your supernatural life

Holy Communion preserves and increases the supernatural life of your soul. In the Holy Eucharist, Christ becomes present so that He may abide bodily among us by His Real Presence in our tabernacles, renew the Sacrifice of Calvary in an unbloody manner on our altars, and nourish our souls in Holy Communion.

The Eucharist is not only a sacrifice, but a sacrament as well. As a sacrifice, it relates in the first instance to God; as a sacrament, to ourselves. Through the Blessed Sacrament God bestows upon us the grace by which we obtain supernatural life and are saved.

By the imparting of divine grace, God has made it possible for us to share His own nature and His own vital activity. The life of God calls for appropriate food. The Bread of Angels has become, through transubstantiation, the food of man. This Bread, the product of our Savior's love and power, is the only food that is worthy of the Father who gives it and the adopted children who receive it from His hands. It produces wondrous effects in those children. The first and principal effect is that it gives divine life to the soul.

Holy Communion is the Body of Jesus under the form of bread, received as food. With His Body, He gives also His Soul, His divinity, His merits, and His grace. All that He is, all that He has, He makes your own. No being on earth is richer and more honored than you are when you bear in your heart your God and Savior. You could not ask for more. Christ could not give you more.

Because Jesus Christ Himself is the very essence of this sacrament, it follows that the Holy Eucharist is the most sublime and greatest of all sacraments, not only in dignity but also in power. Holy Communion is the most intimate union of ourselves with Christ, and therefore it must excel all other sacraments in power to sustain and increase the supernatural life within us. It is justly called the Blessed Sacrament.

In order to appreciate Holy Communion, you must understand its effects. Nine effects in particular will be considered.

∞

Through the Eucharist, you share in the life of God

God is the source of life. From all eternity the Father gives Himself to the Son. Together the Father and the Son give themselves to the Holy Spirit, sharing with Him Their one divinity.

The eternal Son of God, in His limitless love for our fallen race, became incarnate that men might have life, and might have it more abundantly.[81] At the time of the Incarnation, most of the children of Adam had ceased to live the supernatural life and had devoted themselves to the pursuit of vain honors, deceitful riches, and sinful pleasures. They had ceased to recognize the glorious dignity to which they were called — that of children of God — and had sunk to the lowest depths of sin.

The only-begotten Son of God then condescended to become man so that He might raise man to God. He descended to the depths of humiliation so that He might raise man to a most exalted dignity, to the sharing of God's own life. It was not enough for Him to offer to God's offended majesty that atonement which only a

---

[81] Cf. John 10:10.

divine Person could adequately pay and to merit for man the supernatural life Adam had forfeited, but in His undying love for men, Jesus bequeathed to us a marvelous gift that was to feed and foster the supernatural life within our souls, adorn them with holiness, and thus perfect us more and more in our glorious dignity of divine sonship. This wondrous gift is the living Flesh and Blood of the Word Incarnate, substantially present in the consecrated Host.

Christ not only bestowed on us His life-giving Flesh and Blood, but He even threatened with everlasting perdition those who would refuse to nourish their souls with this heavenly Bread.[82]

The reception of the Blessed Sacrament is of supreme importance to every soul Christ has redeemed. According as that heavenly banquet is rightly partaken of, or neglected, man will enjoy throughout eternity the fulfillment of the supernatural life in the Beatific Vision of God, or will be excluded from Him.

God wants to give you a share in His divine life. Before doing so, however, He gave His life in all its fullness to the sacred humanity of Jesus because of its union with the second Person of the Blessed Trinity. This divine life then extends from Christ, the Head, into the Body of the Church. The members of this Body are the faithful who in turn share in that intimate life of the three Divine Persons.

Christ is the Mediator through whom grace comes to all men. By His sacrifice on the Cross, He has merited this divine life that mankind had lost by sinning. Jesus gives you His divine life and unites you with God through the sacraments, especially in Holy Communion, for it is the sacrament of union.

St. Augustine prays, "Other priests offered for themselves and for their people; this Priest, not having sin that He should offer for Himself, offered Himself for the whole world, and by His own Blood entered into the holy place. He, then, is the new Priest and

---

[82] Cf. John 6:53.

the new Victim, not of the law but above the law, the universal Advocate."

∞

The Bread of Life is food for your soul

The first effect of Holy Communion is life. All the sacraments either impart supernatural life to the soul or develop it in the soul where it is already found. They do this for certain purposes. For instance, the sacrament of Penance raises the soul from death to life; Confirmation bestows on it a special strength to fight against its external enemies. But the Eucharist is concerned with the supernatural life itself. Its function is to intensify and strengthen that life. St. Thomas writes, "We should consider the effects of the Eucharist with regard to the manner in which the sacrament is conferred, as it is given in the form of food and drink: thus all the effects that material food and drink produce for the corporal life — that is, to sustain, to cause growth, to repair loss, and to delight — this sacrament produces them also for the spiritual life."

Holy Communion is a sacrament, and hence, like all the other sacraments, it is a sign instituted by Christ to give grace. Like all the other sacraments, Holy Communion also is designed to give that precise grace of which it is a sign. Baptism, for example, is a symbolic bath; it contains and confers the grace of spiritual cleansing from sin. Confirmation is an anointing; it brings with it the grace of spiritual maturity. It makes its recipient firm in the Faith, anointed for the spiritual battle like an athlete of old.

Holy Communion is a sign of nourishment; hence, it is meant to bring to the soul the graces of spiritual nourishment. Holy Communion is meant to do for the soul what material food does for the body, and that is to preserve life and protect it. Material food enables you to continue living and protects you from fatal disease; Holy Communion preserves the spiritual life of your soul and protects you from the spiritual disease of mortal sin.

In His discourse after the multiplication of the loaves, Jesus stresses this fact five times. "I am the living Bread which came down from Heaven; if any one eats of this Bread, he will live forever; and the Bread which I shall give for the life of the world is my Flesh. . . . Unless you eat the Flesh of the Son of Man and drink his Blood, you have no life in you; he who eats my Flesh and drinks my Blood has eternal life, and I will raise him up at the last day."[83] The sharing of divine life means that God lives in you and you in Him, and that as God the Son has by nature the same life as the Father in its infinite fullness, so you share it by grace.

Our Lord compared the Most Holy Sacrament of the Altar with the manna given to the Jews, because the Holy Eucharist was intended to be the daily spiritual food of Christians, just as manna had been the daily food of the Israelites in the desert.

Manna is like the eucharistic Bread, the Body and Blood of our Lord, which comes from Heaven to feed our souls during our life on earth, until we arrive at last in Heaven, our eternal home, the land of promise. Jesus said, "I am the Bread of Life. Your fathers ate the manna in the wilderness, and they died. This is the Bread which comes down from Heaven, that a man may eat of it and not die."[84]

It is in the midst of a meal, under the form of food, that Jesus chose to institute the Eucharist. He gives Himself to you as the nourishment of your soul: "My Flesh is food indeed, and my Blood is drink indeed."[85] In the Our Father, he taught us to say, "Give us this day our daily bread." This refers to Holy Communion. Like the manna, the Eucharist is bread come down from Heaven to give life by nourishing grace within your soul. The life of your soul is supported and developed by eating the "Bread of Life," much in the same way as the life of your body is supported by eating your

---

[83] John 6:51-54.
[84] John 6:48-50.
[85] John 6:55.

ordinary meals. Just as it is necessary to supply your body with food every day, so you must nourish and feed your soul, since obviously the soul has no less need of spiritual nourishment than the body has of material nourishment.

Jesus has prepared for you this great feast of the Holy Eucharist — the food of the soul. If you receive Communion only seldom, you become a prey to temptation and sin, and, growing weaker spiritually, you may fall into mortal sin. Many Catholics have good health and are blessed with the material goods of this world. They are very much alive physically, but are dead spiritually.

Therefore, Jesus comes not only to visit you in Holy Communion, but to be the food of your soul, that receiving Him you may have life — the life of grace here below, the life of glory hereafter.

∞

The Eucharist gives you sanctifying grace

Sanctifying grace is that grace which gives your soul new life, that is, a sharing in the life of God Himself.

Sanctifying grace makes your soul holy and pleasing to God. Sanctifying grace makes you live the life of God, especially by increasing divine love in your heart. Love makes you most like God; thus, love of God through sanctifying grace makes you truly happy.

Sanctifying grace makes you an adopted child of God. In you, as a Christian, have been fulfilled the words of St. John: "But to all who received Him, who believed in His name, He gave power to become children of God; who were born, not of blood nor of the will of the flesh nor of the will of man, but of God."[86]

Sanctifying grace makes you a temple of the Holy Spirit. At the Last Supper, Jesus said, "I will pray the Father, and He will give you another Counselor, to be with you forever."[87] And St. Paul wrote

[86] John 1:12-13.
[87] John 14:16.

to the Corinthians, "Do you not know that you are God's temple and that God's Spirit dwells in you?"[88]

Sanctifying grace gives you the right to Heaven. Just as your soul is the life of your body, so sanctifying grace is the life of your soul. You need sanctifying grace to save your soul. Mortal sin brings death to your soul, because it takes away sanctifying grace, and this means losing God Himself and becoming a child of the Devil. This is the greatest evil that is caused by mortal sin.

To understand why the Church incessantly stresses the desirability and advantages of receiving the sacraments frequently, particularly the Holy Eucharist, you have but to recall her doctrine concerning sanctifying grace. The possession of this "God-life" in your soul is the only consideration that will be of importance at the end of your life upon earth. The degree of happiness enjoyed by each one in Heaven will depend only on the degree of sanctifying grace in the soul on entering eternity.

Now, the chief means of increasing grace are prayer and the sacraments. Each time you receive any sacrament with the right disposition of soul, you receive an increase of divine life. There are but two sacraments that may be received frequently: Penance and the Eucharist. Of these the chief is the Eucharist, since in it Christ Himself is received. It follows that the closer you approach to being a daily communicant, the more logical use do you make of one of the chief means of grace.

∞

The Eucharist enables you to live in Jesus

The Eucharist, as a sacrament, produces in you an increase of habitual, or sanctifying, grace by its own power. Its effects are like those of food: it maintains, increases, and repairs your spiritual forces, causing also a joy that is not necessarily felt, yet it is real.

[88] 1 Cor. 3:16.

Holy Communion not only preserves the life of your soul, but increases it, just as the body is not only supported by means of natural food, but increases in strength.

Holy Communion also preserves and increases all the various virtues, which are bestowed upon your soul together with sanctifying grace. By increasing the theological virtues (faith, hope, and charity), Holy Communion enables you to enter into closer union with God, and by strengthening the moral virtues (prudence, temperance, justice, and fortitude), Holy Communion enables you to regulate better your whole attitude toward God, your neighbor, and yourself. By rendering the seven gifts and the twelve fruits of the Holy Spirit[89] more abundant, Holy Communion opens your understanding and will to the inspirations and promptings of the same Holy Spirit.

The Holy Spirit sanctifies souls by the supernatural gift of grace. The highest type of grace is sanctifying grace, which is a spiritual quality, dwelling in our soul, making it like God Himself. Our Lord spoke of the reception of this life as a spiritual birth when He said to Nicodemus, "Unless one is born anew, he cannot enter the kingdom of God."[90]

Sanctifying grace is also called habitual grace, because once we have received it, it remains as a habit in our soul. Once it has been received, sanctifying grace remains in the soul unless it is driven out by mortal sin.

The Holy Spirit is the skillful gardener. The root of the vine is the sinful soul. Through grace the Spirit gives it His divine life so that it may blossom forth into virtues.

---

[89] The gifts of the Holy Spirit are wisdom, understanding, counsel, fortitude, knowledge, piety, and fear of the Lord. The fruits of the Holy Spirit are charity, joy, peace, patience, kindness, goodness, generosity, gentleness, faithfulness, modesty, self-control, and chastity.

[90] John 3:5.

Before our Lord went forth to His Passion, He left to His Apostles and to us all a last testament in His parting discourse. When His bodily presence had to be taken from us, He earnestly and repeatedly enjoined, "Abide in me."[91]

The bond uniting Him and you can be only a spiritual one, yet it is something real and living, something enduring, not passing, and rooted in the very essence of your being. He used the significant parable of the vine and branches to illustrate: "I am the vine, you are the branches. He who abides in me, and I in him, he it is that bears much fruit, for apart from me you can do nothing. If a man does not abide in me, he is cast forth as a branch and withers; and the branches are gathered, thrown into the fire and burned."[92]

The stem and the branches are one same being, nourished and acting together, producing the same fruits because fed by the same sap. In the same way Jesus and the faithful are united in one Mystical Body. He makes the sap of His grace to spring up within you, especially by means of Holy Communion, and thereby increases and develops the divine life of your soul.

Pope Pius XII in his encyclical letter on the Mystical Body of Christ says, "In the Holy Eucharist the faithful are nourished and strengthened at the same banquet and by a divine, ineffable bond are united with each other and with the Divine Head of the whole Body."[93] You will be able to say with St. Paul, "It is no longer I who live, but Christ who lives in me; and the life I now live in the flesh I live by faith in the Son of God, who loved me and gave Himself for me."[94]

To have sanctifying grace is the first, most essential, and abiding condition of union with Christ, and the basis of all gifts and

---

[91] John 15:4.
[92] John 15:5-6.
[93] *Mystici Corporis*, sect. 19.
[94] Gal. 2:20.

powers that make up the spiritual life. This grace is a real, spiritual, and abiding faculty of your soul, a partaking in the divine nature and image of the divine Sonship in a spiritual manner, so that you become like Christ, who is the Son of God by nature. As long as sanctifying grace remains in you, He is and remains within you that you may be one in Him and in the Father, as They are one. "That they may all be one; even as Thou, Father, art in me, and I in Thee, that they also may be in us."[95] The Father and the Son are one by the possession of the same divine nature. You possess an image of that nature in sanctifying grace.

St. Cyril of Jerusalem[96] wrote, "With full assurance let us partake as of the Body and Blood of Christ: for in the figure of bread is given to thee His Body, and in the figure of wine His Blood; that thou by partaking of the Body and Blood of Christ, may be made of the same Body and the same Blood with Him. For thus we come to bear Christ in us, because His Body and Blood are distributed through our members; thus it is that, according to blessed Peter, 'we become partakers of the divine nature.' "

Surely you ought to be eager to go to Holy Communion often in order not to lose life everlasting. This is the greatest loss possible, for the smallest degree of sanctifying grace is worth more than anything that the world can offer. Even the greatest earthly happiness is nothing in comparison with that of possessing sanctifying grace and eternal life in God. Look into your soul, for Heaven's beginning is there in the form of grace.

---

[95] John 17:21.
[96] St. Cyril (c. 315-386), Bishop of Jerusalem.

Chapter Ten

∞

Seek union with God

The second effect of Holy Communion is union. The union of Christ and your soul is fulfilled and completed in Holy Communion. Not only do you cling to Him by faith, not only are you incorporated into Him through Baptism, but this is a new union that is most real and most spiritual. This union with Christ is symbolized by the sacramental sign. For if Jesus has willed to give Himself to us under the form of food, it is because He wishes to enter into the closest possible union with us. Nothing can be more intimate than the union that exists between the living body and the food it transforms into its own substance.

This union is so intimate that Jesus does not hesitate to say, "As the living Father sent me, and I live because of the Father, so he who eats me will live because of me."[97] This is not merely a moral union based on the fact that you and Christ share the same sentiments of love, but a real physical union that implies that you share in the very life of Christ.

The basic instinct of love is to seek union. The human heart craves the presence of what it loves. It was a longing for union with our souls that filled the Sacred Heart of Jesus when He said to

[97] John 6:57.

His disciples at the Last Supper, "I have earnestly desired to eat this Passover with you before I suffer."[98]

Jesus said, "This is my body which is given for you. Do this in remembrance of me"[99] and "Lo, I am with you always, to the close of the age."[100] Jesus leaves the world, and yet He continues to abide in the world. Not only does He remain with us in a way that cheats the conditions of space and time; He wills even to be in us, for each Host consecrated on the altar is meant to find its resting place in the tabernacle of a Christian heart. There God is united with His creature and His child.

We were created for union with God, which finds its fulfillment in the glory of the Beatific Vision. This vision is begun here below in Baptism and is prefigured in the Eucharist. The direct instrument of this union with God is the Holy Eucharist. Baptism, sacrifice, Communion: that is the sequence in the attainment of life with God. By Baptism, we are born to the supernatural life, becoming members of the Mystical Body of Christ. As members of that Body, we are in a position to offer God a sacrifice that is agreeable to His divine majesty.

Sacrifice adapts your soul for the union with God that is reached in Holy Communion. The degree of union is in the measure of your sacrifice. The more complete the renunciation of all that is contrary to the divine life in you, the greater is the reception of the divine life and the closer your likeness to God.

∞

The Eucharist unites you with Christ's sacred humanity
When you receive Holy Communion, you receive the real and physical Body and Blood of Christ, together with His Soul and His

[98] Luke 22:15.
[99] Luke 22:19.
[100] Matt. 28:20.

divinity, veiled under the appearance of bread. Your soul is like a temple in which Christ lives and where the angels adore Him.

This union with Jesus is so intimate and sacred that it is called *Holy* Communion. When you receive the consecrated Host, you enjoy the unspeakable honor of a visit from the Lord who is God Almighty Himself and at the same time the Man Jesus Christ. Hidden under the appearance of bread is the same Jesus who spoke to people, blessed little children, and healed the sick. You can bring home to yourself this wonderful fact and come to appreciate it more deeply only if you meditate quietly on the words of the Gospel and on the inspired teaching of the Church on the Holy Eucharist.

∽

The Eucharist unites you with Christ's divinity

You share in Christ's divine life as the Divine Word, as the only Son of the Father. You receive the life the Father gives to the Son from all eternity. Therefore, Holy Communion gives you the whole Christ — His Body, Blood, Soul, and divinity. You can possess His divinity in your soul at all times by remaining in the state of grace. But it is only at the time of Holy Communion that you enjoy the great privilege of being intimately united with the human nature of our Lord.

God has poured forth all the treasures of His wisdom and holiness on the sacred humanity of Jesus Christ because of its union with the Divine Word. The measure of His gifts to you is the degree of your union with the same Word. Now, this union with the Divine Word is effected by the power of the sacred humanity, especially in Holy Communion. You must try to keep yourself in a habitual state of adoration and submission to the Divine Word, who resides in you. If you reach this state of submission, your soul will become the object of God's best gifts.

To receive our Lord in Holy Communion is the most wonderful thing that can happen to you, because it means having the infinitely great God in your own heart. How great must be His love for you to stoop so low to reach you! St. John Chrysostom writes, "By Communion we are united to Him whom the blessed spirits dare not behold, so penetrated are they with holy reverence. We become one body, one flesh with Him. Where is the shepherd who nourishes his flock with his own blood? We see many mothers who confide their children to nurses. It is not thus Jesus Christ does in our regard: He nourishes us with His own Blood."

By Baptism man is built up into a spiritual dwelling, which St. Paul calls "the temple of God."[101] Through Confirmation, with its fullness of grace, this dwelling is solemnly consecrated as a temple of the Holy Spirit. Finally, in the sacrament of the Holy Eucharist, the King of Glory Himself enters into that temple and dwells and reigns in it as the soul's most honored Guest. Thus, the Eucharist is the crowning of the spiritual life of the soul.

St. Thomas Aquinas says, "Baptism is the beginning of a spiritual life and the door to the other sacraments, but the Eucharist is the consummation of the spiritual life and the end purpose of all the sacraments. Holiness, which other sacraments produce in the soul, is but the preparation for the reception and consecration of the Eucharist. Thus the reception of Baptism is necessary to spiritual life, but the reception of the Eucharist is necessary for its consummation, that is, to its final complement and perfection."[102]

∽

The Trinity becomes your Guest

Holy Communion brings about a special union with the Three Divine Persons of the Holy Trinity. In virtue of the indwelling of each Divine Person within the other, the Divine Word does not

---

[101] Cf. Eph. 2:21-22.
[102] *Summa Theologica*, III, Q. 73, art. 3.

come alone into your soul. He comes with the Father forever generating His Son; He comes with the Holy Spirit forever proceeding from the mutual embrace of the Father and the Son. Jesus said, "If a man loves me, he will keep my word, and my Father will love him, and we will come to him and make our home with him."[103]

The Three Divine Persons are already in you by grace, but at the moment of Communion they are present within you because of another special title. As you are then physically united to the Incarnate Word, the Three Divine Persons also are, through Him and by Him, united to you, and They love you now as They love the Word-Made-Flesh, whose member you are. When you carry Jesus in your heart, you also bear the Father and the Holy Spirit with Him. Thus Holy Communion is a foretaste of Heaven.

Eucharistic Communion is the most perfect act of our divine adoption. There is no moment when you are more justly entitled to say to the heavenly Father, "Our Father." You abide in His Son, and His Son abides in you. This divine Son, proceeding from the Father, receives the communication of His divine life in its fullness. Faith tells you that you have received His Son in Communion. At that moment, you are with the God-Man, and since you share in His life, the heavenly Father beholds you in Jesus, through Jesus, and with Jesus as the Son in whom He is well pleased.

Thus by sanctifying grace, the entire Trinity is the Guest of your soul. Yet this is, if possible, more true at the moment of Communion, because Jesus comes to you as the Bread of Life, expressly to bestow upon you that life which He receives from His Father. At Communion your soul becomes, as it were, the heaven of the Blessed Trinity.

[103] John 14:23.

Chapter Eleven

∞

Be transformed into Jesus

Through Holy Communion, Jesus abides in you by His grace and the action of His Spirit. He says, "Abide in me, and I in you."[104] *To abide* expresses perfect union. Jesus comes to you to live within your soul, to be the life of your soul, so that He may transform you, little by little, into Himself. The special effect of Holy Communion is to make you Christlike, not only by giving you sanctifying grace, but also by giving you actual graces to preserve His divine life in your soul.

Actual grace is a supernatural help of God that enlightens your mind and strengthens your will to do good and avoid evil. Actual grace lasts only during a certain action. It is a free gift that God bestows upon you when you need it. Actual grace helps you to act as you should. You cannot do good unless God helps you with His grace, for Jesus said, "Apart from me you can do nothing."[105]

Each of the sacraments also gives a special grace, called sacramental grace, which helps us to carry out the particular purpose of that sacrament. With sanctifying grace is given the right to special actual graces that enable us to obtain the purpose for which the

---

[104] John 15:4.
[105] John 15:5.

sacrament was instituted. This sacramental grace is given according as circumstances demand — that is, when we need it, not only at the time we receive the sacrament.

The spiritual union with Jesus can be as lasting as you want it to be, for Jesus said, "He who eats my Flesh and drinks my Blood abides in me, and I in him."[106] Jesus wants to remain with you always. With the help of His grace, you can always be united with Him. After the sacramental Species have disappeared, the Soul of Jesus departs from you together with His Body, but His divinity remains with you as long as you are in the state of grace. In fact, His sacred humanity, united to His divinity, maintains a special union with your soul.

The Body of Christ comes to you to establish more perfectly the spirit of Christ in you. The spirit of Jesus is the Holy Spirit. Each Communion is made in order to establish His dwelling in you more intimately. He takes in hand the ordering of your life. He gives light to your mind; He gives strength and courage to your will.

The Holy Spirit, who dwells within the human soul of Jesus, remains in you, too, in virtue of the special relationship you have entered into with Jesus Christ by sacramental Communion, and produces in your soul dispositions like those of the holy Soul of Jesus. At the request of Jesus — whose prayers for you are unceasing — the Holy Spirit grants you more abundant and more efficacious actual graces. He preserves you from temptations, strengthens your will, and enkindles your love. Thus this divine Spirit directs your soul and its faculties by His grace and continues within your soul the effects of Holy Communion.

St. Paul tells us, "He said to me, 'My grace is sufficient for you, for my power is made perfect in weakness.' I will all the more gladly boast of my weaknesses, that the power of Christ may rest

---

[106] John 6:56.

upon me."[107] You may be weak, but through Holy Communion the strength of Christ fills your soul. Jesus has promised that through Holy Communion not only shall we abide in Him but He will also abide in us. That is the strength of Christ. The more your life flows from Him, the more you have the strength of Christ, and the more it glorifies the Father. For Jesus said, "By this my Father is glorified, that you bear much fruit, and so prove to be my disciples."[108]

In his encyclical letter on the Mystical Body of Christ, Pope Pius XII states, "As then in the sad and anxious times through which we are passing there are many who cling so firmly to Christ the Lord hidden beneath the eucharistic veils that neither tribulation, nor distress, nor famine, nor nakedness, nor danger, nor persecution, nor the sword can separate them from His love (Rom. 8:35), surely no doubt can remain that Holy Communion, which once again in God's Providence is much more frequented even from early childhood, may become a source of that fortitude which not infrequently makes Christians into heroes."[109]

You receive Jesus so that you may be strengthened. Each day brings a cross of some kind, and you need strength to bear it bravely. You will procure strength from your union with Christ in Holy Communion. By sanctifying grace and by Holy Communion, you are intimately united to Christ, and this union must bear fruit in your daily life.

Try to make your life daily more Christlike. Try to think, speak, and act in accordance with His divine will. Your Communions will not dispense you from the conflict. The Devil may even tempt you more fiercely, just because you are striving to lead a higher life; but if you go on bravely struggling, in the end you will conquer. There will be falls, but they will be less and less deliberate. As long

---

[107] 2 Cor. 12:9.
[108] John 15:8.
[109] *Mystici Corporis*, sect. 84.

as you are doing your best to serve God fervently, you can approach the altar of God with confidence and humility. There you will find strength and help in time of need, and, if you are in earnest, you cannot fail to profit by your Communions.

When a temptation assails you, when you feel urged to say an unkind word or to do an action unworthy of a friend of Jesus, remember that you have received Communion that day, and this will help you to hold firm and to resist the Devil. If you are called upon to make some sacrifice, and you hesitate and are ready to refuse, make this sacrifice as a preparation for your Communion tomorrow.

If you live up to your Communions, you will surely make progress in holiness. If you cannot arrive at the degree of holiness to which the saints have attained, at least you can try to follow their example in your feeble measure. The Holy Eucharist is your great source of strength. When you are called upon to conquer yourself, remember that if God asks you to sacrifice something for love of Him, He will, at the same time, give you the grace to obey. He who has strengthened His saints will also help you in your hour of need.

∞

Communion transforms you

The third effect of Holy Communion is transformation. When food is assimilated to the living organism, it has a twofold function to fulfill: it gives growth to the body and repairs the losses of energy and substance sustained in the tension of daily life. In natural life, the living being gives its own form to the nourishment it takes. In the supernatural life, the divine food transforms to itself the person who partakes of it.

In Holy Communion, there exists between Jesus and you a union like that of food and the one who eats it, with this difference: Jesus transforms you into Himself; you do not transform Him into your substance. St. Augustine expressed it this way, putting these words on the lips of our Lord: "I am the food of great souls; grow and you shall be able to eat of me. But you shall not change me into yourself as you do material food; it will be you who shall be changed into me."[110] This union tends to subject the flesh more and more to the spirit and to make it more chaste. This union sows in the flesh the seed of immortality: "He who eats my Flesh and drinks my Blood has eternal life, and I will raise him up at the last day."[111]

St. Dionysius of Alexandria[112] wrote, "As fire reduces to its own state all things with which it comes in contact, and communicates itself to all that comes near it, in like manner the Lord our God, who is an ardent fire, makes us become, through that sweet nourishment, the perfect images of Himself by transforming us into Him."

St. Thomas Aquinas uses two similes to illustrate this. If a drop of water is distilled in a large vessel filled with wine, it is changed into wine. In a similar way, the noble affections and the great virtues of Jesus work upon your heart and form it to divine ideals, so that your thoughts, words, and actions bear the stamp of the child of God. Your soul begins to be like Christ.

Or, when a cutting from an excellent, fruitful tree is grafted onto a wild, uncultivated one, it causes the uncultivated tree to produce fruits that have the good qualities of the graft. So Jesus, grafted, as it were, onto your weak human nature, corrects its defects and gives it His own goodness. As a result, you bear, through Him, leaves, flowers, and fruits such as He bears Himself. If no obstacles are put in the way, the life of Jesus becomes yours; His interests become yours; your will reflects His. In a word, His spirit lives in you. It works in you to produce its crowning and most characteristic effect: divine charity. Jesus said, "He who abides in me, and

---

[110] *Confessions*, Bk. 7, ch. 10.

[111] John 6:54.

[112] St. Dionysius (d. 265), Bishop of Alexandria.

I in him, he it is that bears much fruit, for apart from me you can do nothing."[113]

This union with Jesus in Holy Communion is spiritual and most transforming. The soul of Christ unites with yours to make you but one heart and one mind with Him.

Christ's imagination and memory, so righteous and holy, unite themselves to your imagination and memory to discipline them and turn them toward God and the things of God. You are more inclined to remember God's numerous benefits, His thrilling beauty, and His limitless goodness.

Christ's mind, the true light of the soul, enlightens your mind with the light of faith, enabling you to see and value all things as God sees and values them. Then you realize the vanity of worldly goods and the folly of worldly standards, as well as the wisdom and beauty of the Gospel truths. Little by little, your thoughts, your ideas, your convictions, and your judgments undergo a change. Instead of weighing the worth of things with the world's standards, you make the thoughts and the views of Jesus Christ your own. You lovingly accept the maxims of the Gospel. You continually ask yourself the question: What would Jesus do if He were in my place?

Christ's will, so strong, generous, and constant, comes to correct your weakness, inconstancy, and selfishness by communicating to your will its own divine energy. You can then say with St. Paul, "I can do all things in Him who strengthens me."[114] You feel now that the effort to strive for virtue and to resist temptation will become easier, since you are not alone. You share in the power of Christ Himself. His Sacred Heart, aglow with love for God and for souls, comes to enkindle your own, which is often so cold toward God and so attracted to creatures. The disciples of Emmaus felt

[113] John 15:5.
[114] Phil. 4:13.

this love. "Did not our hearts burn within us while He talked to us on the road?"[115] Under the action of this divine fire, you feel the impulse of grace to do good, to undergo all sufferings for God and to refuse Him nothing; and you want to persevere in doing these things because your heart is filled with divine love.

This union also affects your desires and your choices. Realizing that self is inconstant and uncertain and the principles of the world are often contrary to those of Christ, in whom alone truth abides because He is the Eternal Wisdom, you begin to desire nothing except what He desires — that is, God's glory, your own salvation, and that of your neighbor. You want only what He wants, even as He wanted only what His Father willed. Even when this holy will nails you to the cross, you accept it with all your heart, certain that it aims at your spiritual welfare and that of your neighbor.

Your heart, also, gradually frees itself from its selfishness, from its lower natural affections and attachments so that it may love God and souls in God more earnestly. You learn to love God Himself rather than the consolations He offers. The grace of this union makes you live a more intense supernatural life. Self no longer lives, thinks, and acts, but Jesus Himself, His spirit, lives within you and gives life, as St. Paul said, "It is no longer I who live, but Christ lives in me."[116]

It is especially through prayer and the sacraments, and above all through actual graces given during and after Holy Communion, that Jesus helps you to practice virtue and become like Him. The coming of Jesus to you tends to establish between His thoughts and yours, between His will and yours, such a oneness that you have no other thoughts, no other desires than those of Jesus, as St. Paul says, "Have this mind among yourselves, which is

[115] Luke 24:32.
[116] Gal. 2:20.

yours in Christ Jesus."[117] Inasmuch as you are united with Christ, they are common to you and Him. You love God with the Heart of Christ; you praise God with the life of Christ; you live by His life. He lives in you to work through you, not only in church, but at home, at school, in the shop or office, and at recreation, so that you may be Christlike in your thoughts, desires, words, and actions.

Wherever you are, you are a member of Christ, a Christ-bearer. Through you He continues His life on earth, for you represent His life in the world. Through you His light must shine, His example must radiate, and His life must spread for the glory of God and the salvation of souls. The divine presence of Jesus and the sanctifying influence of His grace should penetrate so intimately your whole being, both body and soul, with all their powers, that you become "another Christ."

∞

Develop the spiritual life you received at Baptism

You have at your disposal four great means of sustaining and expanding the spiritual life God has so graciously granted you through Baptism, so that you may give yourself wholeheartedly to God as He has given Himself to you.

* *Fight relentlessly and fearlessly against your spiritual enemies:* the world, the flesh, and the Devil. With the help of God's grace and the aid of your heavenly protectors, you may be assured of certain victory and the further strengthening of your spiritual life.

* *Sanctify all your actions by offering them frequently to God.* You will thereby acquire many merits, add to the degree of sanctifying grace, strengthen your title to Heaven, and make reparation for your sins.

[117] Phil. 2:5.

♦ *Pray much,* since prayer keeps you in touch with God at any time of the day or night. After the sacraments, prayer is the richest channel of grace. Pray much and you will receive much grace.

♦ *Receive the sacraments frequently.* When received with right and fervent dispositions, the sacraments add to your personal merits a rich bounty of grace that proceeds from Christ's own merits. By approaching frequently the sacrament of Penance and receiving Communion, even daily, if possible — or at least on Sunday — you will have the power to become a saint. Jesus said, "I came that they may have life, and have it abundantly."[118]

St. Thérèse wrote, "The best means to reach perfection is through receiving Holy Communion frequently. Experience sufficiently proves it in those who practice it."

Your task is to lay your soul open to receive this divine life, to foster it and make it grow by your constant sharing in the dispositions, virtues, and sacrifices of Jesus Christ, until you can say with St. Paul, "It is no longer I who live, but Christ who lives in me."

The nature of the Christian life is a real sharing in God's life, for God lives in you and you in Him by grace. He lives in you in the unity of His nature and in the Trinity of His Persons. He is active there, creating in your soul a supernatural organism that enables it to live a life, not indeed equal to, but truly like His — a Godlike life. He gives your soul light and strength by His actual grace, helps you to make your acts meritorious, and rewards them by a further infusion of sanctifying grace.

You also live in God and for God, for you must cooperate with His grace. By the aid of His grace, you freely accept His divine impulse, cooperate with it, and by it triumph over your enemies,

[118] John 10:10.

acquire merit, and prepare yourself for the grace given to you by the sacraments. Even your free consent to accept His grace is the work of His grace.

Christ instituted the sacrament of the Eucharist precisely in order that He might unite Himself to each one of us as the source of all life, strength, light, and spiritual fruitfulness. Hence, Jesus comes first of all to unite us to Himself as members to their Head, in one Mystical Body. All the other fruits of the sacrament flow from this one, which is the most important. This is the chief reason for the Real Presence of Christ in the Eucharist.

The Body of Christ that you receive in Holy Communion is the living Body of the Incarnate Word. Since this Body of Christ comes to you filled with the power and the reality of the Divine Word and of the Holy Spirit, you are intimately united to the Divine Word and filled with the Holy Spirit.

In coming to you in Holy Communion, Jesus wills to fill you with the same Holy Spirit of love with which He is filled Himself. He wishes in this way to make you share in the divine life and to transform you entirely in Himself. This is the whole meaning of the Eucharist.

In his encyclical letter on the sacred Liturgy, Pope Pius XII describes our union with Christ in the Eucharist: "The very nature of the Sacrament demands that its reception should produce rich fruits of Christian sanctity. . . . Therefore let us all enter into the closest union with Christ and strive to lose ourselves, as it were, in His most Holy Soul, and so be united to Him that we may have a share in those acts in which He adores the Blessed Trinity with a homage that is most acceptable and by which He offers to the eternal Father supreme praise and thanks which find a harmonious echo throughout the heavens and earth, according to the words of the prophet: 'All ye works of the Lord, bless ye the Lord.' "[119]

[119] *Mediator Dei* (November 20, 1947), sect. 124, 127.

In the sacrament of the Eucharist we have the Body of Christ present as the cause of our sanctification, since on the altar He makes present the redeeming Sacrifice of Calvary.

When you realize the fact that Christ not only gives grace to us but also gives Himself in this sacrament, you can understand why you are led to the highest sanctification through Holy Communion. This sacrament is given to you not only to help you imitate Christ, but so that you may be another Christ. It identifies you with Christ. St. Thomas says that confirmation brings us an increase of grace in order to resist temptation, but the Eucharist does even more: it increases and perfects our spiritual life itself, in order that we may be perfected in our own being, our own personality, by our union with God.

Our Lord made consoling promises to those who abide in Him. If you are united to Him as the branches are to the vine, you "shall bear much fruit," your prayers will be heard and answered, your joy shall be full, you will be "the friend" of Christ, and you will live by Him. All these precious promises are contained in the very words of our Lord in St. John's Gospel.[120] This union with Christ is to be effected and perfected daily more and more by Holy Communion.

When St. Francis de Sales was asked why he went so often in Holy Communion, he replied, "I often speak with my teachers because I can learn much from them. Jesus is the teacher of the science of holiness. I go to Him because I would like to learn from Him how to become a saint. Of what use to me is all knowledge and education, if I do not become holy?"

---

[120] John 15:5-15.

Chapter Twelve

Let Communion fill you with divine love

The fourth effect of Holy Communion is divine love. This sacrament most fittingly tends to the love of man for God, because it was begun and inspired in the love of God for man. St. John points to that love when he says, "When Jesus knew that His hour had come to depart out of this world to the Father, having loved His own who were in the world, He loved them to the end."[121] Then the Evangelist goes on to tell that the Savior gave us the Eucharist to show this love. The love of His Sacred Heart discovered the wonderful mystery of the union that could henceforth be effected unceasingly on the altar.

Jesus once said, "I came to cast fire upon the earth; and would that it were already kindled!"[122] Through the Holy Eucharist, Jesus casts fire into men's hearts. He Himself is that flame of love.

The Sacred Heart of Jesus ardently longs to communicate to us His own charity. He said to St. Margaret Mary, "My Divine Heart is possessed of such a burning love for men and for you in particular that, unable to contain the flames of its burning charity, it must needs extend them through you, that it may be made known to

[121] John 13:1.
[122] Luke 12:49.

them in order to enrich them with its priceless treasures." He then asked the saint for her heart in order to unite it to His own and place in it a spark of His love. He does this in an ordinary way for us in Holy Communion and every time we unite our hearts to His.

Sanctifying grace, which you receive through Holy Communion and which attaches itself to the very essence of your soul, brings with it supernatural powers and faculties that enable you to perform virtuous deeds. The most important of these is the virtue of charity, by which you love God above all things for His sake, and your neighbor as yourself for the love of God. St. Thomas Aquinas says, "Primarily and essentially, the perfection of the Christian life consists in charity."

At Holy Communion, Jesus is within you with all His most pure and holy love. So often you lament that your love is tainted with selfishness, and you long to love God intensely, as He deserves. Yet in spite of your efforts, you love Him so little. Here is the immense, inexpressible love you need — most holy, perfect, free from self. You possess Jesus, Love itself, in your heart.

Heed the advice of St. Francis de Sales: "Your principal intention in Communion should be to advance, strengthen, and console yourself in the love of God: for you ought to receive for love's sake that which love alone causes to be given you."[123] Where can you more appropriately offer love for love to our Savior than in the Most Holy Sacrament, which is rightly called the Sacrament of Love?

∽

Christ appeals for your love

St. Bernard[124] once wrote, "What is it that God requires of us? Our heart can offer nothing more worthy than to give itself back

---

[123] *Introduction to the Devout Life*, Pt. 2, ch. 21.
[124] St. Bernard (1090-1153), Abbot of Clairvaux.

to Him who made it, and this God demands from us when He says, 'Son, give me thy heart.' "

Jesus longs for your love. Give Him your whole heart and your whole love. This love is a gift that comes from Him, and it is in Communion that He gives it.

If you yield yourself up every morning — or at least on Sunday morning — without reserve to Jesus in Holy Communion, He will be your Master in the spiritual life. He alone knows what you need, and if you place yourself at His entire disposal, He will do the rest. The spiritual life is simple, like God Himself, once Jesus is the whole life of your soul. Renew your baptismal promises each day; then take the risen life of Jesus as the model of your life, and all will go well.

It is wonderful to see how St. Thérèse yielded herself to the action of this flame of love of the Sacred Heart. Describing her First Communion she writes, "How sweet to my soul was the fond caress of Jesus. It was a caress of love. I felt that I was cherished very much and I said, 'I love You; I give myself to You for all time and eternity.' Jesus asked nothing of me; He claimed no sacrifice. For, long since, both He and His little Thérèse had contemplated each other and had understood each other. On that day, however, our encounter could not be called a simple look. It was a fusion of two spirits. We were no longer two. Thérèse had disappeared like a drop of water lost in the ocean; Jesus alone remained. He was Master and King. And straightway the joy of Thérèse became so great and so overpowering that it could no longer be contained. Tears silent and full of sweetness began to flow."

The only obstacle to this complete reign of Christ in you is your selfishness. You must die to your selfish life in order to live in the divine life. The Christ-life in you is a life of self-surrender, of love. Love yields your will to Christ, and through it, your whole being and all your energies. Christ gives Himself to you according to the measure of your love. If you are detached both from yourself and creatures, if you give yourself to Him unreservedly with a pure heart, Jesus in exchange gives Himself to you as only God is able to do. St. John has said, "God is love, and he who abides in love abides in God, and God abides in him."[125]

If you yield to the working of His grace, you will find your mind and will be more ready to do what Jesus inspires you to do. If you do not put obstacles in the way of God's grace, and if your fervor in receiving Holy Communion continues, the life of Jesus will manifest itself more distinctly in you.

Pope Pius XII wrote, "Wherefore, since the Heart of Christ overflows with divine and human love, and since it is abundantly rich with treasures of all graces which our Redeemer acquired by His life and His sufferings, it is truly the unfailing fountain of that love which His Spirit pours forth into the members of His Mystical Body. It [devotion to the Sacred Heart of Jesus] demands the full and absolute determination of surrendering and consecrating oneself to the love of the Divine Redeemer. The wounded Heart of the Savior is the living sign and symbol of that love. It is likewise clear, even to a greater degree, that this devotion especially declares that we must repay divine love with our own love."[126]

Try to lose yourself in this ocean of love of the Heart of Jesus. Admire in silence His wonderful love for His Father and for all men, and cling to this limitless love that is now yours. Try to find in Him your delight, and let Him cleanse all the stains of your self-love. Let your poor cold heart, which loves so little, be subjected to the transforming influence of the tremendous love of the Sacred Heart of Jesus so that you may become one with Him.

---

[125] 1 John 4:16.
[126] *Haurietis Aquas*, sect. 6, 85.

Chapter Thirteen

∞

Learn to love others

Holy Communion is the banquet of love Christ has prepared for the children of God. It is not surprising, then, that our Lord, immediately after having given the first Communion to His disciples, declared the great commandment of love: "A new commandment I give to you, that you love one another; even as I have loved you, that you also love one another. By this all men will know that you are my disciples, if you have love for one another."[127]

St. Ignatius of Loyola[128] wrote, "To love our neighbor in charity is to love God in man, and man in God; it is to hold God alone dear for His own sake, and the creature for the love of Him." The Eucharist is the bond of charity that unites all Christians as members of one spiritual body, the Church, even as the soul gives life to each member of the human body. St. Paul says, "The bread which we break, is it not a participation in the Body of Christ? Because there is one bread, we who are many are one body, for we all partake of the one bread."[129] Jesus is that Bread in Holy Communion.

---

[127] John 13:34-35.

[128] St. Ignatius of Loyola (1491-1556), founder of the Jesuit Order.

[129] 1 Cor. 10:16-17.

The Catholic Church is called the Mystical Body of Christ because her members are united by supernatural bonds with one another and with Christ, their Head, thus resembling the members and head of the living human body. St. Paul teaches that the Church is a living body with Christ as its Head. "Now, you are the body of Christ and individually members of it."[130] Just as each member of the body receives vital power from the head, so we, if we are living members of the Church through sanctifying grace, are constantly receiving the supernatural power of grace from Christ, our Head. Thank God every day for giving you the grace of being a member of the one true Church.

In a radio address on the twenty-fifth anniversary of his episcopal consecration, May 13, 1952, Pope Pius XII declared, "Whence did the courageous faith of the early Christians derive its life and enthusiasm? From the eucharistic union with Christ. . . . At the Table of the Bread of the Strong they felt themselves united in fraternal union by one same love, welded together in a mystic bond that makes thousands of hearts and thousands of souls one great family with but one heart and one soul."

In his encyclical letter on the Mystical Body of Christ, he wrote, "The sacrament of the Eucharist is itself a striking and wonderful figure of the unity of the Church, if we consider how in the bread to be consecrated many grains go to form one whole, and that in it the very Author of supernatural grace is given to us, so that through Him we may receive the spirit of charity, in which we are bidden to live now no longer our own life but the life of Christ, and to love the Redeemer Himself in all the members of His social body."[131]

Holy Communion is set apart from the rest of the sacraments, because it contains not only grace, but also the Author of grace

---

[130] 1 Cor. 12:27.

[131] *Mystici Corporis*, sect. 83.

Himself, Jesus Christ. In all other sacraments, Christ makes a visible sign the means of grace; in the Sacrament of the Altar, He makes use of His own Body as the instrument of grace. This explains certain effects of Holy Communion. For instance, Holy Communion, besides protecting and preserving our Christian life of grace, is also meant to unite us with Jesus Christ Himself and with the members of His Mystical Body, who are our neighbors, in a union of supernatural charity.

In Holy Communion, you enter into union directly with Jesus Christ and, through Him, with the Father and the Holy Spirit, who are in Him. You also enter with Him and through Him into union with all members and especially with those who are perfectly united with Him in glory.

It is necessary that we know and love Christ as He really is. The real Christ is the *whole* Christ, the Mystical Christ — the Head and the members.

The sacrament of the Eucharist imparts to you as a sacramental grace that fervor of charity by which you can, if you make good use of it, unite yourself more firmly to Christ and to your brethren.

St. Augustine says, "O Sacrament of true piety, sign of unity, bond of charity . . . The Lord had given us His Body and Blood under the species of bread and wine, and as the bread is made out of many grains of wheat and the wine from many grapes, so the Church of Christ is made out of the multitude of the faithful united by charity."

Through Holy Communion we realize that blessed state for which Christ prayed to the Father: "That they may be one, even as we are one."[132] If the spirit of Christ is to dominate the masses, and peace, happiness, and charity are to prevail in each family, then let them go often to Holy Communion, and their example will work wonders. The Lord's Supper is the unity of the Body of Christ, not

[132] John 17:11.

117

only in the Sacrament of the Altar, but in the bond of peace. A complete transformation of society is possible only if Catholic men, women, and children receive the Eucharist in greater numbers. If they fall off from receiving the sacraments, all the bonds of family and social life give way, and they run the risk of being scattered by the materialistic spirit of our age.

∽

Communion is a remedy for unkindness

Through frequent Holy Communion, Jesus will give you help to carry out His great commandment of love for your neighbor and to put away all unkindness. He will give you the grace to love your neighbor as yourself for His sake; to respect and love him as God's image and likeness, as a child of your heavenly Father, as the temple of the Holy Spirit, as one to whom He gives Himself in Holy Communion, as one whom He identified with Himself when He said, "As you did it to one of the least of these my brethren, you did it to me."[133] You cannot be unkind to one whom Christ loves and for whom He died on the Cross.

St. Francis de Sales wrote, "Jesus as our Lord has always preferred us to Himself, and does so still as often as we receive Him in the Blessed Sacrament, making Himself therein our food; so in like manner He wishes us to have such a love for one another that we shall always prefer our neighbor to ourselves." Thus, Holy Communion is a remedy for unkindness. With frequent Holy Communion to strengthen you, it will not be so difficult to spend yourself in serving others.

The chief supernatural powers bestowed on your soul with sanctifying grace are the theological virtues: faith, hope, and charity. Charity is the virtue by which you love God above all things for His own sake, and your neighbor as yourself for the love of God.

[133] Matt. 25:40.

To give yourself to Jesus Christ is to give yourself to others for love of Him, or, rather, to give yourself to Him in the person of your neighbor. Our Lord never gives Himself except to those who give themselves to Him in the person of their neighbor. For as God is incarnate in the holy humanity of Jesus Christ, He is in some manner incarnate in your neighbor. As you can go to God only through this sacred humanity, you can be united to Christ only by accepting Him united to your neighbor.

Yield yourself up to Jesus without fear so that He may work in you all that the interests of His glory demand. He comes to you in Holy Communion in order to change you into Himself. Let this eucharistic life be a continual model of charity for you. In the Mass, Jesus is a Victim immolated to the glory of His Father and given over as food to His brethren. You, too, should try every day to be more and more a victim immolated to the glory of the Blessed Trinity and a victim of charity immolated to souls by expiation and to your family and neighbor by patience, kindness, and cheerfulness. Forget yourself to think of the interests of God and your neighbor.

By frequent Holy Communion, learn to overcome your selfishness; learn to resist your natural feelings and reactions, such as hatred and bitterness; develop kindness and sympathy, forbearance and forgiveness; learn to think kindly of everyone and to find your happiness in making others happy; and thus you will unite yourself by charity with Christ and with His members in His Mystical Body.

By uniting all the faithful with Jesus, Holy Communion unites them with each other in charity. We should, therefore, take to heart the admonition of St. Augustine: "Let all this avail us to this end, that we eat not the Flesh and Blood of Christ in the Sacrament, as many evil men do, but that we eat and drink to the participation of the Spirit, that we abide as members of the Lord's Body to be quickened by His Spirit."

Chapter Fourteen

Gain protection from sin

Mortal sin is the greatest evil in the world, because it drives out of your soul the divine life of sanctifying grace and turns you away from God, the source of all life, peace, and joy. But our Lord protects your soul from mortal sin by giving you more sanctifying grace in Holy Communion, God's very life in your soul. "Unless you eat the Flesh of the Son of Man and drink His Blood, you have no life in you."[134]

Through Holy Communion you also receive actual grace, which gives you the light to see what is evil and the strength you need to fight against it. In this way, your soul is strengthened against temptation. "This is the bread which comes down from Heaven, that a man may eat of it and not die."[135]

Just as bodily food repairs what you lose by daily wear and tear, so likewise this divine food is a remedy for the spiritual infirmities of each day. Ordinary food is medicinal as well as nourishing, and so is Holy Communion. As those who are ill should visit the doctor and take his medicine, so also the Catholic who feels his own weakness and is fearful of being unable to persevere in well-doing

---

[134] John 6:53.
[135] John 6:50.

is the one person above all others who has need of frequently, even daily, receiving the Body of Jesus Christ.

Jesus is the Physician of your soul who can keep you from the spiritual death of mortal sin and cure you of the spiritual sickness of venial sin. But if you ignore the Savior and neglect Holy Communion, your soul will remain spiritually sick. Take advantage of the visit of Jesus in Holy Communion so that He may preserve your soul from the greatest evil in the world: sin.

St. Ignatius of Loyola said, "One of the most admirable effects of Holy Communion is to preserve souls from falling, and to help those who fall from weakness to rise again; therefore, it is much more profitable frequently to approach this Divine Sacrament with love, respect, and confidence than to keep back from an excess of fear and cowardice."

Those who make a practice of receiving Communion frequently try to avoid whatever might lead them into sin. Should they fall into serious sin, they usually try to get to Confession as soon as possible. As time goes on, they advance in grace and their falls become less frequent; they are at peace with God. Thus, St. Ignatius adds, "Of the gifts of grace which the soul receives in the Eucharist, one must be counted among the highest; the Eucharist does not allow the soul to remain long in sin or to persist in it obstinately."

∞

Purity comes through Holy Communion

The sacramental effect of Holy Communion, which is traced to the physical contact it establishes between Christ and us, is the lessening of our inordinate desire for sexual pleasure. Sex and the pleasure which is involved with sex are good and holy things. Yet, since the Fall, we find ourselves drawn to an unlawful pursuit or enjoyment of this pleasure.

One of the sacramental effects of Holy Communion is gradually to rectify this disorder. Christ, looking upon our bodies as part of His own Mystical Body, will watch over them with a special providence, and will be more eager to help in times of temptation to control and weaken these inordinate desires.

St. John Chrysostom writes, "The mystical Blood chases the Devil far away and attracts to us the King of Angels with His celestial armies; the demons flee at the sight of that divine Blood, while the angels fly to our aid."

Our Lord once said to St. Mechtilde,[136] "The oftener a person washes himself with water, the cleaner he will be. The oftener a person receives Communion, the more I will live in him and he in me, and the purer his soul will become. The oftener the depth of my divinity penetrates his soul [through frequent Holy Communion], the more it will be expanded and become capable of receiving my divinity."

Pope Pius XII has stated, "It is the Eucharist which lessens the ardor of passions, increases the fire of charity, gives a man a detachment from lowly things, and heads him toward high and heavenly things."

Holy Communion is needed most of all by those who are weak and struggling to break some sinful habit. It is the most powerful remedy against temptation and the greatest influence in freeing one from the evil tendencies of human nature. The Council of Trent says, "In the holy mysteries there is power to preserve us pure and unhurt from sin as it were by a heavenly medicine, against the easy approach and infection of deadly disease. . . . It also restrains and represses the lust of the flesh; for while it inflames souls with the fire of charity, it necessarily puts out the fires of passion."

St. Thomas Aquinas teaches, "Although this sacrament is not directly ordained to diminish concupiscence, it diminishes it as a consequence by an increase of charity, because, as St. Augustine says, an increase of charity is a decrease of cupidity. It [charity]

---

[136] St. Mechtilde (c. 1241-1298), Benedictine nun.

directly confirms the heart of man in virtue, by which he is preserved from sin."

St. Cyril of Alexandria[137] says, "When Jesus Christ is in us, He appeases the revolts of our flesh. He strengthens our piety and extinguishes the passions of our soul."

Young couples preparing for marriage should frequent the Table of the Lord. Through the Sacrament of Love, they will learn to love unselfishly. Their purity is protected by the life-giving food of the soul. Since all, young and old, find this inclination to evil within themselves, they need to look with confidence for help to Jesus Christ in Holy Communion.

The Church recommends frequent Communion to the young who are tempted to sins of impurity. The Catholic Church is the only institution that offers the means to moral recovery, and her greatest means is frequent Holy Communion. The coming of Jesus in Holy Communion awakens new love in the hearts of youth and encourages them to love purity and sinlessness — necessary conditions for happiness.

Cardinal Newman[138] wrote, "It is the boast of the Catholic Church that it has the gift of making the young heart chaste; and why is this, but that it gives Jesus Christ for our food, and Mary for our nursing Mother?" St. John Bosco[139] made splendid men of some 200,000 boys, of whom 8,000 became zealous priests. He used to say, "I know only two educational instruments: Holy Communion and the rod, and I have given up the rod and use only Holy Communion."

One of the chief effects of Holy Communion is the lessening of our inclinations to sin. In the decree of Pope Pius X on frequent

---

[137] St. Cyril (d. 444), Patriarch of Alexandria.

[138] John Henry Newman (1801-1890), noted English convert to the Catholic Church.

[139] St. John Bosco (1815-1888), founder of the Salesian Order.

Communion, we read, "The desire of Jesus Christ and of the Church that all the faithful should daily approach the Sacred Banquet is directed chiefly to this end, that the faithful, being united to God by means of the sacrament, may derive from it strength to resist their sensual passions, to cleanse themselves from the stains of daily faults, and to avoid those graver sins which they may commit through human weakness; so that the main purpose of Holy Communion is not that the honor and reverence due to our Lord may be safeguarded, nor that the sacrament may serve as a reward of virtue bestowed on those who receive it. . . . 'Holy Communion is the remedy whereby we are delivered from daily faults, and preserved from mortal sins.' "

Holy Communion is the most effective remedy and protection against the temptations that press round about you on every side. You need fear nothing if Christ is with you. By His actual graces, He will strengthen your soul, so that you may courageously resist all evil. He will not permit any serious sin ever to separate you from Him. He will strengthen you against even lesser sins that would weaken your friendship if you let Him work in your soul by the sacramental graces of frequent Holy Communion. One Holy Communion should be enough to make your soul holy and sinless, and yet, after many Communions, you may not have succeeded in correcting your faults. Perhaps it is because you have not received Holy Communion with greater fervor and sufficient frequency.

At Communion Jesus is within you with all His admirable purity. Think of that when temptations assail you, sometimes painfully, and when you feel despondent over your lack of ability to resist them. Rejoice in the perfect, spotless purity Jesus brings with Him, and plead for the grace to imitate it in some measure.

You will never perfectly understand the infinite charm of that chastity that delights the angels and created the Immaculate Heart of Mary and all the holy virgins. But all that purity is yours in Holy Communion. Love this purity that is the source of all created purity. Into its unfathomable depths throw the world with its innumerable varieties of guilt and, above all, your own guilt.

This life is, in a certain measure, also a sharing in Mary's life. She shares in a very special degree in His dispositions and virtues. Since He wills that His Mother be also our Mother, He wills that she engender in us this spirit. Giving us spiritual life — as a secondary cause, of course — Mary makes us share not only in the life of Jesus, but also in her own, in the life of Jesus living in her.

∞

Holy Communion remits venial sin

Holy Communion also takes away venial sin, provided you are sorry for it and you have no affection for it or desire to commit it in the future. You may sometimes doubt your sorrow and fervor. It will console you to remember that the minimum disposition will suffice to obtain forgiveness when you add to it the sacramental power of Holy Communion.

After mortal sin nothing is more terrible than venial sin. It really offends God's infinite majesty and brings upon you the punishments of Purgatory. It banishes true joy from your heart, because it draws you away from God, your highest good. Venial sin is an ugly stain that makes your soul displeasing in God's sight. It hinders Him from enriching you with so many more graces that could help you to love and serve Him better.

Venial sins can be forgiven by Holy Communion — not directly, but indirectly — by the power of the acts of love this sacrament inspires. The Council of Trent calls it "a remedy by which we are freed from our daily faults." In the same manner, some of the debt of temporal punishment due to sins already forgiven is taken away by a worthy Communion. Even your daily deliberate venial sins become less numerous with frequent Communion.

Chapter Fifteen

∞

Increase the power of your prayer

No prayer can be more effective than that said after Holy Communion, when Jesus is present in your heart as God and man, as your best Friend, ready to help you by means of the many graces He wishes to grant you. He helped people in His day, because they had faith. Receiving Holy Communion is the best evidence that you can give of your faith. If God is to hear prayer, it must proceed from an innocent heart, and a person is never more careful to keep his soul free from sin than when Christ comes to purify his heart.

Jesus Himself said that your heavenly Father will give you whatever you ask in His name: "Amen, amen, I say to you: if you ask the Father anything in my name, He will give it to you."[140] So there is nothing that you may not hope to receive when, at Holy Communion, Christ prays in and with you to His Father in Heaven. But at the Last Supper, Jesus expressly promised to hear your prayer on the condition that you abide in Him through Holy Communion, when He said to the Apostles, "If you abide in me, and my words abide in you, ask whatever you will, and it shall be done for you."[141] It is especially by Holy Communion that you

[140] John 16:23 (Douay-Rheims version).
[141] John 15:7.

abide in Him, for He also said, "He who eats my Flesh and drinks my Blood abides in me, and I in him."[142]

What can God refuse you when He makes Himself your own? God will keep His word. After placing all your difficulties in your Savior's hands, you may look forward to the future with firm confidence. There is no friend so faithful, no one so ready to help you as our Lord, and He is the Author and Source of all graces. He loves you more than anyone else ever can. He is interested in giving you the graces you need to save your soul, because He died for it.

When offering your Holy Communion for someone else, either a living soul or a soul in Purgatory, remember that this does not mean that you can transfer to another the sacramental effects of Holy Communion, for these are always restricted to the one who receives the sacrament. But the prayers that you recite before and after Holy Communion possess the power to move God to grant favors and the power to make satisfaction for temporal punishments, and these values can be transferred to others. Moreover, by Holy Communion, you can always gain indulgences that may be applied to the souls in Purgatory.

∞

Make a novena of Holy Communions

It should be clear then that since the sacraments are God-given means of grace, and the Holy Eucharist the greatest and holiest of the sacraments, no novena can be more fruitful than a novena of Holy Communions. You may receive Holy Communion on nine consecutive days of the week, or on nine consecutive Sundays in petition for a special favor. Then you may make another novena of Communions immediately afterward in thanksgiving, even if you have not received the favor you prayed for. Even if your prayer was not answered, you will have drawn closer to God and

---

[142] John 6:56.

received the graces that accompany each Holy Communion. The sanctification of your soul is the greatest favor you could obtain through Holy Communions.

Sometimes God will not answer your prayer at once in order to test your faith. Perhaps He chooses to grant you something else that He considers more necessary for you, or He may grant you something better. You will never go wrong letting God grant an answer to your prayers in His way, not your way, for He knows what is best for you. In making a novena of Holy Communions, resignation to God's will must be absolute, as is the case with any prayer you say.

No definite prayers are necessary in order to make a novena of Holy Communions. What really matters is that you receive Holy Communion with deep faith and love and rely on the promise Jesus made after the Last Supper: "If you abide in me, and my words abide in you, ask whatever you will, and it shall be done for you." Perseverance in presenting your request in the course of one or many novenas is very important. Perseverance has the sanction of our Lord, for He also promised, "Ask, and it will be given you; seek, and you will find; knock, and it will be opened to you. For everyone who asks receives, and he who seeks finds, and to him who knocks it will be opened."[143] All this indicates perseverance in prayer, which is the purpose of any novena, and one of the conditions necessary if one's petitions are to be answered.

It is good to remember that if you are receiving Holy Communion on nine Sundays, you need not go to Confession before each Holy Communion (although it is very good to do so) unless you are sure you have committed a mortal sin. Venial sins should not keep you from receiving; make an act of perfect contrition and approach the Holy Table without fear. It is advisable, however, to go to Confession at least every two or three weeks.

[143] Matt. 7:7-8.

Chapter Sixteen

Find joy and consolation

Holy Communion is the feast of the soul — that is to say, a source of deepest joys. As bread imparts to the body strength and a feeling of contentment, so does the Bread of Life bring peace and joy to your heart because of the wonderful fruits of grace it produces in your soul.

St. Thomas Aquinas says, "This Bread of Angels, containing in itself all delights, satisfies by an admirable virtue the taste of all those who receive it worthily and with devotion; it satisfies better than the manna of the desert and surpasses the relish of all sensual pleasures."

The glorious Christ who comes to you hidden under the sacramental species is the same Christ who, having redeemed and sanctified us, will be our everlasting joy in Heaven.

At Holy Communion, there is opened to you a world of life, light, and love, a gracious outpouring of the treasures of the Sacred Heart of Jesus, the Fount of all grace, holiness, and Christian joyfulness. At this fount of joy you will find the strength and courage to undertake great things for God's glory and the welfare of your neighbor.

Heaven is the possession of God in all His glory and beauty; therefore, since Holy Communion is the possession of that same

God, although veiled under the sacred elements, it follows that Holy Communion is a foretaste of the joys of Heaven.

Try to form some idea of the heavenly joy that unceasingly wells up in the soul of Jesus, who is within you in Holy Communion with all His infinite bliss. Perhaps sometimes in the past you have felt spiritual consolation and peace, like a foretaste of the joys of Heaven. Multiply such happiness a thousand times more than you can imagine; it is still nothing compared with the bliss that fills the soul of Jesus.

Like the Father, Jesus is infinitely perfect, and this fills Him with infinite joy. Each of His divine perfections — His beauty, wisdom, holiness, love, mercy, and power — is for Him an object of loving contemplation that overflows into inexpressible joy. The love He has for the Father, and His Father's love for Him, flood His Sacred Heart with indescribable happiness that will be our admiration and bliss for eternity.

Pope Pius XII begins his encyclical letter on devotion to the Sacred Heart with these words, which give the letter its title: " 'You shall draw waters with joy out of the Savior's fountains' (Isa. 12:3). . . . Those heavenly blessings which devotion to the Sacred Heart of Jesus pours into the souls of the faithful, purifying them, refreshing them with heavenly consolation and urging them to acquire all virtues, cannot be counted."[144]

Jesus is in the Sacred Host to share His divine perfections and happiness with you. He gives you there His limitless, most perfect love, that it may fill you with joy and destroy your self-love. He brings you His infinite bliss so that, forgetting yourself and your troubles, you may find all your happiness in Him and thus enjoy on earth a foretaste of His heavenly joys.

What more do you need than Jesus to make you perfectly happy? He is your treasure, your only good, who is all you should

---

[144] *Haurietis Aquas*, sect. 1, 2.

want to love in this world. He is and always will be perfect, and perfectly happy. You should rejoice in this ocean of joy and peace of the Sacred Heart.

But to enjoy His divine perfections more, you must love more, rise above self, and live more in Him than in yourself. Ask Jesus to help you with His grace so that you, too, may sometimes experience something of what the saints felt before the tabernacle, or when they took Him to their hearts in Holy Communion.

What joy to think that you possess within you and take to your heart all the beauty, wisdom, goodness, love, holiness, and happiness there is in Heaven and on earth! What is there in Heaven or on earth that you could wish for, that you do not possess in possessing Jesus?

But this joy is above all spiritual. Since the Eucharist is the "mystery of faith," it may happen that God will not permit this inward joy to react upon your feelings. If you have brought all the good dispositions possible for receiving Christ, and still feel helpless, remain in peace. Christ acts in silence but surely, in the innermost depths of your soul in order to transform it into Himself. That is the most precious effect of this heavenly food. The more often you receive Christ in the sacrament of His love, the better will you understand how sweet the Lord is.

This spiritual joy brought to you by Holy Communion will make you bear the trials and sufferings of life with a peaceful, contented heart. You are enabled to imitate, in some measure, the mysterious experience in the life of Jesus — the union of intense agony and intense happiness.

His words to the Apostles are fulfilled in you through Holy Communion: "So you have sorrow now, but I will see you again and your hearts will rejoice, and no one will take your joy from you."[145] At Communion you see Him with eyes of faith and your

[145] John 16:22.

133

heart rejoices. This is the true, lasting joy that neither the world nor the powers of evil can take from you.

The moments of union with Jesus in Holy Communion are the happiest of your life, for this union of love is the climax of God's love for you. Your heart is filled with heavenly bliss, because God Himself makes it His little heaven of delights when He visits you in Holy Communion. Yearn to be with Him and to possess Him here on earth through frequent Holy Communion, and you will prepare yourself for an eternal union with Him in Heaven. At Holy Communion you enjoy a foretaste of Heaven, for you receive Christ's glorified Body and Blood, Soul and divinity, and His Sacred Heart is the fount of joy.

⚭

Holy Communion will console you

Holy Communion will also afford you great consolation in all the sorrows and sufferings of this earthly life. No matter how great your need and your trouble may be, no matter if all forsake you, Christ will never fail you. How could you doubt Him who became man and died on the Cross for you and who gave Himself to be your daily food?

During His earthly life, Jesus was ever kind and compassionate. You may hope for everything from Him in Holy Communion, since you take Him into your heart. He will be your best comforter and helper. He invites you to Holy Communion with such gentle tenderness: "Come to me, all who labor and are heavy laden, and I will give you rest."[146]

If your heart is often sad, it is because you may be looking for consolation and happiness in creatures, forgetting that lasting peace and comfort come from God. True peace and consolation spring from divine love. Sin is the cause of all unhappiness and

[146] Matt. 11:28.

misery in this world, since it deprives souls of God's friendship. St. Augustine wrote, "Our hearts were made for Thee, O Lord, and they are restless until they rest in Thee."[147] You cannot rest in God more surely than through Holy Communion.

[147] *Confessions*, Bk. 1, ch. 1.

Chapter Seventeen

Prepare for Heaven

"O Sacred Banquet, in which Christ is partaken of, the remembrance of His Passion is cherished, the mind is flooded with grace, and a pledge of future glory is given unto us." This beautiful prayer bursts forth from the heart of the Church as she replaces in the tabernacle the consecrated Treasure entrusted to her keeping. It expresses God's teaching regarding the most beautiful mystery of our holy Faith.

The glory that is reserved for us in Heaven is twofold: the glory of the soul and the glory of the body.

The glory of the soul consists in the Beatific Vision of God. God communicates to the soul a wondrous gift known as the light of glory, whereby His own splendor pervades the human mind and empowers it to see God as He sees Himself. By the light of glory the human soul gazes upon God's unveiled truth, goodness, and beauty; it sees God face-to-face and drinks in eternally the divine perfections. As a result of that vision, the soul is borne unto God by the irresistible impulse of beatific love, is thrilled with indescribable sweetness.

Like a piece of iron placed in a blazing fire until it becomes white-hot, almost transformed into fire, although remaining iron, so it is with the soul in Heaven. It is plunged into the sea of God's own glory, immersed in the ocean of uncreated light and splendor, transformed, as far as possible, into the very Godhead, while remaining a created thing.

Second, there is the glory of the body — a supernatural gift whereby our frail bodies are rendered like the glorified body of our risen Savior. On the last day, the bodies of the just will be brilliant like the sun, endowed with the power of angelic swiftness, spiritualized, and impassible.[148]

The glory of the body results, in a sense, from mere contact with the glorified soul, like the clouds at sunset, radiant with the splendor of the sun that bursts through them. Our bodies will be resplendent in eternity with the glory of the soul that will radiate through them. Throughout our Savior's life, a constant miracle was necessary in order to conceal or suspend the glory that should have shone forth from His sacred Body united to His deified Soul; so the Transfiguration on Tabor[149] was but a glimpse of the Lord's beauty.

Thanks to our Savior's grace, to His love and mercy, you can attain that everlasting glory. You have been given in this life a pledge of sharing in the glory of our Redeemer: the glorified Soul and Body of Jesus Christ in the adorable Eucharist. The Blessed Sacrament is the pledge of, and the preparation for, the eternal glory of the soul and of the body.

What consolation you will derive at the hour of death from the thought of having received Communion frequently! Your soul, being brought so closely into contact with your Savior, has shared in His divine life, has eaten His Flesh and drunk His Blood, so that you enjoy a pledge of everlasting life, for He said, "I am the living Bread which came down from Heaven; if anyone eats of this

---

[148] Impassibility is the state of being beyond the reach of suffering or harm.

[149] Matt. 17:1-2.

bread, he will live forever."[150] You will be filled with peace. It will not be hard to die. Even though, at the last hour of your life, the Devil will do his utmost to make you lose courage and force you to rebel against God, you may depend upon the graces of Holy Viaticum,[151] the heavenly food of Holy Communion. Jesus will be your strength.

∽

Mary requests that you receive Communion

A striking proof that Jesus and Mary are deeply concerned about your receiving Holy Communion often is the fact that they both made a special promise to grant the grace of a happy death to the souls who receive Holy Communion. When Jesus appeared to St. Margaret Mary and showed her His Sacred Heart, He made His great promise: "I promise thee in the excessive mercy of my Heart that my all-powerful love will grant to all those who go to Holy Communion on the first Friday in nine consecutive months, the grace of final penitence: they shall not die in my disfavor nor without receiving their sacraments; my Divine Heart shall be their safe refuge in this last moment."

Our Lady's great promise during an apparition in 1925 to Lucy, one of the three children to whom she appeared at Fatima, Portugal, in 1917, was: "I promise to help at the hour of death, with the graces needed for salvation, whoever on the first Saturday of five consecutive months, shall confess and receive Holy Communion, recite five decades of the Rosary, and keep me company for fifteen minutes while meditating on the fifteen mysteries of the Rosary, with the intention of making reparation to me." The confession may be made in the eight days before or after Communion. The

---

[150] John 6:51.

[151] Holy Communion given to those in danger of death, thus preparing them for a passage to eternal glory and happiness.

fifteen-minute meditation may be made at any time of the day, either on all the mysteries as a whole or on one special mystery. The Rosary and meditation may be combined by thinking about each mystery a few minutes before or after reciting the decade.

∞

Holy Communion will affect your resurrection

Holy Communion establishes between Jesus Christ and us not merely spiritual contact but physical contact as well through the "species" of bread. The resurrection of the body can be traced from this physical contact with Christ. The resurrected bodies of those who have received the Eucharist during their lifetime will be more strikingly resplendent because of their frequent contact, during life, with the risen Body of their Lord.

The Fathers of the Church in many instances speak of the fact that Christ comes to us in Communion as the source of all life, not only to give us a pledge of future life but also to prepare our soul and bodies for the general resurrection. St. Irenaeus[152] says, "Just as the bread which is produced by the earth hears the invocation of the Holy Spirit and ceases to be bread in order to become the Eucharist, made of two elements, earthly and celestial, so, too, our bodies, receiving the Eucharist, are now no longer corruptible, for they possess the hope of the resurrection."

Although your body will die and be changed to the dust of the earth, it will be reunited to your soul and share its immortality. Jesus said, "I am the resurrection and the life; he who believes in me, though he die, yet shall he live, and whoever lives and believes in me shall never die."[153] The glorious resurrection of the body is an effect of Holy Communion. It confers on you the right to a glorious resurrection, which Christ promised to those who eat His

---

[152] St. Irenaeus (c. 130-c. 200), Bishop of Lyons.
[153] John 11:25-26.

Flesh and drink His Blood: "He who eats my Flesh and drinks my Blood has eternal life, and I will raise him up at the last day."[154]

The bodies of your dear ones have been laid in the stillness of the grave where your own body will be laid someday; nevertheless you will see them face-to-face with the very same eyes and clothed in the same bodies you saw upon earth. This thought should induce you to receive Christ in Holy Communion frequently, even daily. Frequent Communion will multiply and strengthen your own hopes of seeing God in Heaven, with glorified eyes of flesh, and of sitting down there forever with your family and friends to the everlasting banquet prepared for the true and faithful lovers of Christ.

∞

Communion equips you for life

These, then, are the powerful fruits that the Holy Eucharist produces in our souls: life, union, transformation, charity, protection against sin, effective petition, joy, and eternal life. It would perhaps be more accurate to use the singular term *fruit*; for it is but one unique fruit, which is represented to us under different forms, and from different points of view, so that we may understand it better. Charity cannot be understood without transformation, for charity produces this transformation. Transformation cannot be understood without union. None of the three can be conceived without the supernatural life of grace. And all the other effects result from sanctifying grace. Thus, the Eucharist is the crowning of the supernatural life.

St. Thomas Aquinas, the prince of the Church's theologians, sums up the far-reaching effects of Holy Communion: "The sacrament of the Body of the Lord puts the demons to flight, defends us against the incentives to vice and to concupiscence, cleanses the

---

[154]John 6:54.

soul from sin, quiets the anger of God, enlightens the understanding to know God, inflames the will and the affections with the love of God, fills the memory with spiritual sweetness, confirms the entire man in good, frees us from eternal death, multiplies the merits of a good life, leads us to our everlasting home, and reanimates the body to eternal life."

It should be your delight, during your earthly pilgrimage, frequently to receive the heavenly manna, the food of pilgrims, which sustains you in all your trials, preserves and fosters the life of grace within you, and prepares you for everlasting union with our loving Redeemer in our heavenly home. If you turn your eyes away from the false glamour of this alluring world and center all your thoughts and affections on the God of the tabernacle by receiving Him frequently with purity, faith, humility, confidence, love, and desire, then the Holy Eucharist will be for you what Christ intended it to be: the pledge of a glorious resurrection and the foretaste of that beatific life in which you will enjoy the presence of God forever.

∞

Chapter Eighteen

Receive Communion frequently

In order to see how earnestly Holy Mother Church wishes you to receive Holy Communion, let us glance briefly at the history of Holy Communion. In the early days of the Church, it was the common practice for the whole congregation to receive Communion at every Mass. We read in the Acts of the Apostles: "And they devoted themselves to the Apostles' teaching and fellowship, to the breaking of bread and the prayers . . . day by day, attending the temple together and breaking bread in their homes,"[155] wherever the Sacred Mysteries were celebrated.

St. Dionysius of Alexandria wrote, "In the primitive Church, all those who assisted at the consecration of the Eucharist participated in the sacramental Communion."

During the Roman persecution, even when Mass could not be celebrated every day, the faithful enjoyed the privilege of keeping the Holy Eucharist in their homes, giving themselves Communion every morning. The faithful were intensely eager for Holy Communion. All their thoughts seemed to center on the Blessed Sacrament. This practice produced martyrs who would rather die than renounce their religion, despite relentless, bloody persecution.

[155] Acts 2:42, 46.

This went on for three centuries. Like the Christians in the apostolic age, those living in the immediately succeeding centuries approached the Holy Table daily. Gradually, however, this ardent zeal for the reception of the Blessed Sacrament disappeared, and people began to receive Communion less frequently. At first they did so every Sunday, then only a few times a year. But voices were raised in protest, urging all to return to the original custom of the Church, to receive Communion frequently or even daily.

Arius in the fourth century attacked the divinity of Christ. Catholics then, in a bitter struggle against the Arians, preached the divinity of Christ so strongly that they placed very little emphasis on His humanity. Now, when you think of the divinity of Christ, you are naturally impressed with fear and awe. When these fourth-century Christians began to think of Holy Communion in terms of awe and fear only, they came to be very hesitant about receiving. They felt unworthy to receive God, and so they stayed away from the Sacrament.

From that time, many attempts were made to revive the practice of frequent Communion. In almost every century, God raised up saints, such as St. Catherine of Siena,[156] St. Philip Neri, and St. Vincent Ferrer,[157] to preach this means to spiritual health. To some extent they were successful — although the devotion of the early Christians was never equaled — and beginning with the fifteenth century, the practice began steadily to advance.

Then came Jansenism in the seventeenth century. It was a heresy from within that, in spite of condemnation by several popes, influenced the minds of almost all Catholics. The Jansenists, exaggerating again the reverence in which we should hold the Eucharist, laid down such strict regulations for frequent reception that almost no one was considered worthy to receive often. Under their

---

[156] St. Catherine of Siena (c. 1347-1380), Dominican tertiary.

[157] St. Vincent Ferrer (c. 1350-1419), Dominican mission preacher.

influence, piety grew cold, and in many places the average rate of reception fell quickly to the minimum of once a year and less.

∞

Pope St. Pius X encouraged frequent Communion

Although after the first condemnation no one would claim to be a Jansenist, the excessive strictness had infected many, and even learned Catholic teachers and writers disputed among themselves concerning the conditions under which the faithful might be permitted daily or weekly Communion. Then there came a pope who will be known forever in history as the "Pope of the Blessed Sacrament."

From a poor peasant boy he became a humble parish priest, a bishop of a small diocese, the Patriarch of a populous see, and then Pope of the universal Church. He had lived in close contact with his people. He knew their needs; he understood their difficulties; he could discern the approaching clouds of danger that hung over them. Pope St. Pius X was a practical man. He knew the remedy the first Christians used in the Catacombs, which had been forgotten by many. He appealed to the Christian world to turn again to the Blessed Sacrament as the surest hope in this conflict.

Hence, in December 1905, and again in August 1910, he "ordained, commended, counseled, and commanded" two great principles and practices — namely, early Communion for children and frequent Communion for adults. The Church's intention was made clear once and for all when Pope Pius X issued the famous decree on daily Communion, in which he said, with a great deal of proof, that it was ". . . the wish of the Church that all Christians should be daily nourished by this heavenly banquet and should derive therefrom abundant fruit for their sanctification."

The following is a quotation from the encyclical of St. Pius X on frequent Communion: "The holy Synod would desire that at every Mass the faithful who are present should communicate not only spiritually, by a loving desire in their hearts, but sacramentally, by the actual reception of the Eucharist (Council of Trent, sess. 22, ch. 6).

"And this wish of the Council is in entire agreement with that desire wherewith Christ our Lord was inflamed when He instituted the Divine Sacrament. For He Himself, more than once and in no uncertain terms, pointed out the necessity of eating His Flesh and drinking His Blood, especially in these words: 'This is the Bread that has come down from Heaven; not as your fathers ate the manna, and died. He who eats this Bread shall live forever' (John 6:59). Now, from this comparison of the Food of Angels with bread and with the manna, it was easily to be understood by His disciples that, as the body is daily nourished with bread, and as the Hebrews were daily nourished with manna in the desert, so the Christian soul might daily partake of this heavenly Bread and be refreshed by it. Moreover, whereas, in the Lord's Prayer we are urged to ask for 'our daily bread,' the holy Fathers of the Church all but unanimously teach that by these words must be understood, not so much that material bread which is the nourishment of the body, as the eucharistic Bread, which ought to be our daily food.

"Moreover, the desire of Jesus Christ and of the Church that all the faithful should daily approach the Sacred Banquet is directed chiefly to this end, that the faithful, being united to God by means of the sacrament, may derive from it strength to resist their sensual passions, to cleanse themselves from the stains of daily faults and to avoid those graver sins which they may commit through human weakness; so that the main purpose of Holy Communion is not that the honor and reverence due to our Lord may be safeguarded, nor that the sacrament may serve as a reward of virtue bestowed on those who receive it. . . . 'Holy Communion is the remedy whereby we are delivered from daily faults, and preserved from mortal sins' (sess. 13).

"This desire on the part of God [that the faithful should daily approach the Sacred Banquet] was so well understood by the first Christians that they daily flocked to the Holy Table as to a source of life and strength. 'And they continued steadfastly in the teaching of the Apostles and in the communion of the breaking of the bread and in the prayers' (Acts 2:42). And that this practice was to continue into later ages, not without great fruit of holiness and perfection, the holy Fathers and ecclesiastical writers bear witness. . . .

"Frequent and daily Communion, as a thing most earnestly desired by Christ our Lord, and by the Catholic Church, should be open to all the faithful of whatever rank and condition of life; so that no one who is in the state of grace and who approaches the Holy Table with a right and devout intention, can lawfully be hindered.

"A right intention consists in this: that he who approaches the Holy Table should do so, not out of routine, or vainglory, or human respect, but for the purpose of pleasing God, of being more closely united with Him by love, and of seeking this divine remedy for his weaknesses and defects. . . .

"Although it is more expedient that those who communicate frequently or daily should be free from venial sins, especially from such as are fully deliberate, and from any affection thereto, nevertheless it is sufficient that they be free from mortal sin with the purpose of never sinning mortally in future; and, if they have this sincere purpose, it is impossible that daily communicants should not gradually free themselves from even venial sins, and from all affection to them."[158]

∽

The saints encouraged frequent Communion
The writings of the saints in every century bear out the fact that frequent Communion has always been the true spirit of the

[158] *Sacra Tridentina Synodus* (December 20, 1905).

Church. St. Ignatius of Antioch[159] encourages all Christians who are present at Mass to receive Holy Communion: "Come together in common, one and all without exception in charity, in one faith and in one Jesus Christ, who is of the race of David according to the flesh, the Son of Man and Son of God, so that with undivided mind you may obey the bishop and the priests, and break one Bread which is the medicine of immortality and the antidote against death, enabling us to live forever in Jesus Christ."

Origen[160] addresses careless communicants in the following words: "You tell me that you come to church only on feast days; are not the other days festivals too? Are they not also days belonging to the Lord? Among the Jews it is the practice to observe only a few days as festivals . . . but Christians receive the Flesh of the Incarnate Word of God every day."

St. Ambrose[161] encourages daily Communion: "If Jesus Christ is our daily Bread, why do you receive Him so seldom? Live in such a manner that you may be worthy to receive this celestial Bread each day."

St. John Chrysostom advised the faithful of his day as follows: "The time for Communion is not the feast day nor the day for celebrations, but when you have a pure conscience and your life is purified from sin."

St. Augustine stated, "Receive daily what profits you daily; and live so that you may be worthy to receive daily."

St. Bede the Venerable[162] wrote this: "He washes us from our sins daily in His Blood, when the memory of His blessed Passion is renewed at the altar, when the creature of bread and wine is

---

[159] St. Ignatius (c. 35-c. 107), Bishop of Antioch.

[160] Origen (c. 185-c. 254), Alexandrian biblical exegete, theologian, and spiritual writer.

[161] St. Ambrose (c. 339-397), Bishop of Milan.

[162] St. Bede (c. 673-735), biblical scholar.

transferred into the sacrament of His Flesh and Blood by the ineffable sanctification of His Spirit: and thus His Body and Blood are poured out and killed, not by the hands of infidels unto their destruction, but are assumed by the mouth of the faithful unto their salvation."

St. Francis de Sales says, "If worldlings ask you why you receive Holy Communion so often, tell them that it is to learn to love God, to purify yourself from your faults, to free yourself from your miseries, to console yourself under your afflictions. Let two classes of people receive Communion often: the strong, that they may not become weak; and the weak, that they may become strong. . . . Those who have not much worldly business ought to receive often, because they have time to do so, and those who have much worldly business, because they have need to do so. . . . Receive Holy Communion often — as often as you can, with the advice of your spiritual father."[163]

St. Thérèse, perhaps the greatest saint of modern times, writes, "It is not to remain in a golden ciborium that Jesus comes down each day from Heaven, but to find another heaven — the heaven of our soul, in which He takes His delight. . . . It is necessary that the Bread of Angels come like a divine dew to strengthen you and to give all that is wanting to you."

∞

The Church encourages frequent Communion

The true spirit of the Church is daily Mass with Communion. The Council of Trent declared it to be the express wish of the Church "that at every Mass the faithful who are present should receive Communion." This is the Church's ideal, set forth in her history in the pronouncements of the popes and councils, in the writings of the saints, and in the Liturgy itself. The Church speaks

---

[163] *Introduction to the Devout Life*, Pt. 2, ch. 21.

in the name of our Lord through the voice of Pope St. Pius X: "All the faithful, married or single, young or old, even children from their First Communion, are invited to go to Holy Communion frequently; yes, daily." He continues in his encyclical on early Communion for children: "Those who have the care of children should use all diligence, so that after First Communion the children shall often approach the Holy Table, even daily if possible, as Jesus Christ and our Mother the Church desire."

The appeal of Holy Mother Church was addressed to the faithful by her zealous pontiffs, especially Pope St. Pius X and his worthy successors. Pope Pius XII, in his radio address to the National Eucharistic Congress at New Orleans, said, "May we not discern, however, a promise of better things for the Universal Church in the reflowering among you and among all peoples of eucharistic love and the daily increase of an ardent love and devotion for the August Sacrament? While we exhort you from our paternal heart to most holy zeal toward the Blessed Sacrament, we fervently pray with you that, strong in youth, your people, who stand for the wealth and power, may also be a shining example of Catholic faith and Christian virtue."

A genuine Catholic wants the things that Christ wants; for him the will of the Church represents the will of God. And since bad example, evil influence, and temptations to sin surround him daily, he considers it necessary to use Holy Communion frequently, even daily, as his most powerful aid in leading a good life.

When the Church says it is the desire of Christ and her will that they receive Communion often and even daily, what can those Catholics who receive Communion less than once a month say to support their contradictory actions?

Of course, no pope has commanded daily or frequent Communion under pain of mortal or venial sin. Yet there is, no doubt, a large number of Catholics who fall into mortal sin frequently, and who do not receive Holy Communion very often. This is more than a question of urging something solely on the grounds that it makes Catholics more perfect; it has to do with something that ordinarily keeps Catholics from falling into and staying in the state of mortal sin. Therefore, the will of Christ and the Church in regard to frequent Communion cannot be brushed off as mere advice and an invitation to strive for greater holiness. Our Lord's warning must be remembered: "Unless you eat the Flesh of the Son of Man and drink His Blood, you have no life in you."[164]

Normally, the frequency of the worthy reception of the sacrament of the Holy Eucharist is an indication of the state of one's spiritual life. God, of course, will grant the necessary grace and strength to avoid sin and retain the divine life to anyone who, because of circumstances over which he has no control, cannot receive Holy Communion. On the other hand, we certainly cannot expect God to use extraordinary means when we willfully refuse the ordinary ones.

The precept of Easter Communion binds under the pain of sin.[165] However, the Church does not present yearly Communion to us as a desirable standard. By the precept she shows her intention to set it as the absolute minimum that one can do and still be a living member of the Communion of Saints. Those, therefore, possess very little of the spirit of the Church who go to Holy Communion only once or twice a year. They can hardly claim to be good, loyal children of the Church if they do only the minimum that she requires, and do it, moreover, under threats of grievous sin and punishment.

Many call themselves Christians. *Christian* means "follower of Christ," and the substance of Christianity is the life of Christ

---

[164] John 6:53.

[165] The Easter duty requires Catholics to receive the Eucharist at least once a year between Easter and Trinity Sunday (cf. Canon 920).

within us — in our thoughts and in our private and public actions. If such a life is lacking (and how can it be otherwise without frequent Communion?), there remains nothing of Christianity but the name.

May God grant that a great eucharistic age may see every good Catholic at the Holy Table every week, if not daily. But you do not have to wait until then to do what is right. You can begin at once to make Holy Communion your "daily Bread."

Chapter Nineteen

∞

Strive to be worthy
to receive Communion frequently

Holy Mother Church requires two things for frequent Communion: the state of grace — you must be free from every mortal sin, to the best of your knowledge; and a right intention — you should not go to Holy Communion out of mere habit or to be seen by people, but to please God, to be united with Him by love, and to receive this divine medicine for your sins and faults.[166]

∞

To receive Communion, you must be in a state of grace

The wonderful effects of Holy Communion are not wrought in your soul unless it is prepared to receive so many graces. It is true that the sacraments produce fruit of themselves — graces for which they were instituted, but on condition that no obstacle be opposed to their action. There can be none on our Lord's part: in Him are all the treasures of the Divinity, and He infinitely desires to share them with you in giving Himself. The obstacle may then be in

---

[166] Communicants must also fast from food and drink (except water and medicine) for at least one hour before receiving Holy Communion (cf. Canon 919).

you. The Eucharist is the sacrament of union, and the fewer obstacles to this union Christ meets with, the more the grace of His sacrament acts in you. Grave sin, which causes the death of your soul, is the greatest obstacle.

One day our Lord said that the kingdom of Heaven is like a king who made a marriage feast for his son. He sent his servants to call in those invited to the marriage feast, but they would not come. Again he sent out other servants to invite the people, but they paid no attention to them. So the king punished those people. Then the king told his servants to gather all whom they could find and bring them to the marriage feast, because everything was ready. The king went in to see the guests. He saw there a man who had not put on a wedding garment, and he said to him, "Friend, how did you get in here without a wedding garment?" The man did not know what to say. So the king said to his servants, "Bind him hand and foot, and cast him into the outer darkness; there men will weep and gnash their teeth."[167]

The king in this parable is God the Father; Jesus is the Son whose marriage feast is held. The marriage feast is the sacrament of the Holy Eucharist, where you receive the food of your soul. You are invited to receive Holy Communion, but you must have on a wedding garment — that is, you must be in the state of sanctifying grace. If you receive the sacrament in mortal sin, you commit a sacrilege, and God must ask you, too, "How did you get in here without a wedding garment?" If you should die in that state of sin without contrition, He would have to say to the angels, "Bind him hand and foot, and cast him into the outer darkness; there men will weep and gnash their teeth." That would mean eternal punishment.

The first disposition required for Holy Communion is the state of grace. To be in the state of grace does not mean that you must

[167] Matt. 22:12-13.

have been constantly in the state of grace. But at the time you receive, you must be free from grievous sin.

To be in the state of grace does not mean that your conscience must be calm and peaceful, so that, if you have a vague, indefinite fear of being unworthy or of being in the state of sin, you must abstain from Communion. So long as you are not certain of having committed a grievous sin since your last confession, you are worthy to go to Holy Communion.

To be in the state of grace does not mean that you must go to Confession before every Communion. You are obliged to go to Confession before Holy Communion only when you are sure you have committed a grievous sin. It is good to make a practice of going to Confession every week or two; but in case you are unable to get to Confession and are not *certain* of being in the state of sin, make use of the opportunity of going to Holy Communion.

To be in the state of grace means that you must always be free from mortal sin when receiving Holy Communion. The Blessed Sacrament is the spiritual food of the soul, and as natural food cannot benefit a body that is deprived of life, so this heavenly nourishment can produce no effect in a soul that is dead by mortal sin. Should one dare to receive this sacrament while conscious of the guilt of mortal sin, he would stain his soul with the crime of sacrilege and, thus, as St. Paul says, would "eat and drink judgment upon himself."[168] Everyone whose conscience is burdened with mortal sin must, before receiving into his heart his eucharistic God, confess and repent of his sin in the tribunal of Penance.

∞

Receiving Communion requires a right intention
The second disposition required to receive Holy Communion is to have a right intention, which consists in this: that you approach

---

[168] Cf. 1 Cor. 11:29.

the Holy Table not out of routine or to make an impression upon people, or to seek praise, but for the purpose of pleasing God, of being more closely united with Him by love, and of seeking this divine remedy for your weaknesses and failings.

If another human and imperfect motive creeps in — for instance, if you are really prompted by a desire of being better and yet you occasionally have a slight feeling of pride — this does not mean that your intention is no longer right.

You need not express these motives in so many words. The mere fact of receiving Communion freely is proof that you are doing so through faith and confidence in order to become a better Catholic, a holier person, and to love Jesus more. This does not mean that you must have all the right intentions mentioned by the Holy Father.[169] If you have one of them — if you really want to become better — it is sufficient.

The better your dispositions, the more will you profit by the graces of this sacrament. But so long as you have these two dispositions — the state of grace and a right intention — so long as you receive worthily, better an imperfect Communion than no Communion. Every Communion will help you to be better for the following one.

∞

To receive Communion, you must be free of mortal sin

Mortal sin, which causes the death of your soul, is the greatest obstacle to Holy Communion. Mortal sin is a grievous offense against the law of God. It is called *mortal* because it takes away the sanctifying grace that is the life of your soul.

Three things are necessary for a sin to be mortal: grievous matter — the thing must be very bad; full knowledge that it is against God's law — you must know what you are doing; and full consent

---

[169] See excerpts from *Sacra Tridentina Synodus* on page 147.

of your will — you must really want to do it. If one of these three things is missing, there is no mortal sin.

A person who knowingly receives Holy Communion in mortal sin receives the Body and Blood of our Lord, but he does not receive His graces. He commits a very grave sin of sacrilege. A sacrilege is the profanation of sacred objects — and what could be more sacred than Christ Himself? Hence, unworthy Communions often harden the hearts of sinners and cause them to resist grace.

Never go to Holy Communion with a deliberate, unrepented, unforgiven mortal sin on your soul. If you are conscious of being in the state of mortal sin, however contrite you may think yourself to be (even if you are, in fact, contrite), you may not receive Holy Communion without previous sacramental Confession. However, in rare cases, if there is urgent need to receive the sacrament, and if no confessor is available, reception is permissible after an act of perfect contrition is made.

If you remember a grievous sin you have forgotten to confess, you need not confess that forgotten sin before receiving Holy Communion, if at Confession you had sincere sorrow for all your sins, because you are in the state of grace. That sin must be confessed in the next confession if it is remembered. You may continue to receive Holy Communion until the next confession.

∞

Venial sin should not prevent you from receiving

Venial sin is a less serious offense against the law of God. You commit a venial sin when you knowingly and willfully disobey a commandment of God in a less serious matter, or, if the matter was serious, you did not know that what you were doing was seriously wrong or you did not want to do it.

If you receive Communion frequently, it is better to be free from fully deliberate venial sin and from any affection to venial sin. However, it is sufficient to be free from mortal sin with the purpose of never sinning grievously in the future. If you have this sincere purpose, you may be sure that receiving frequently will gradually enable you to free yourself even from venial sins and all attachment to them.

The Church does not make light of venial sin; but at the same time she wants you to remember that venial sin does not involve the death of your soul, nor does it deprive you of God's friendship. Even if your soul is with venial sin, it still remains dear to God through the presence of sanctifying grace. Jesus will surely protect and strengthen the divine life of your soul by His sacramental presence.

If you are conscious only of venial sins, an act of contrition suffices for the worthy reception of Holy Communion. A thousand venial sins do not render a Communion unworthy. On the contrary, contrition with Communion remits venial sins; and frequent Communion is the most powerful medicine to reduce their number.

Do not let the thought of having frequently committed venial sin — in the past or now — keep you from receiving Communion frequently. Receive Communion with humility and contrition, hoping to obtain from this sacrament itself the cleansing of your venial sins and the strength to avoid them in the future.

∞

Temptation differs from sin

A temptation is not a sin. It is an invitation to sin, a fight between your evil desires and your duty to obey God's law. As soon as you decide to give in to your evil desire and want to disobey God's commandments, the temptation is over and you have committed a sin. You must know what you are doing, and you must want to break a serious commandment of God before a mortal sin can be committed. No temptation can harm you as long as you are sincerely seeking to remain in the friendship and love of God.

Doubts may come as to whether you have consented to a temptation. Remember that if you have the habitual will and determination to resist temptation (for example, evil thoughts), and if you have prayed, you may conclude that deliberate consent was lacking. Allow no scruple or doubt to keep you from receiving Holy Communion. Therefore, doubts about whether you are in the state of grace should not keep you from receiving. Make an act of contrition, and receive without any fear.

St. Alphonsus says that in case of doubt, whether or not there are grave reasons for doubt, whether the sin is mortal or venial, a person may go to Communion without previous confession. Simply make a good act of contrition, receive, and then, if you wish, mention the doubtful sin in the following confession. The careless may be advised to confess at least their doubt; habitual sinners should be strongly urged to confess; good, pious Catholics need not confess; the scrupulous ought not to confess.

∞

Go to Confession regularly

Always distinguish between what is necessary and what is more perfect. Confession is necessary for the worthy reception of Holy Communion only if you are conscious of having fallen into a mortal sin — and you must be sure you did — since your last confession. It is more perfect to receive the sacrament of Penance often, preferably every week or two.

There is no obligation to confess unless you are conscious of having committed mortal sin since your last good confession. If you are conscious of mortal sin, however, you should get to Confession as soon as possible, even if some considerable inconvenience is involved.

It is strongly advised that frequent communicants go to Confession once a week to once a month to add the benefits of this sacrament to those of Holy Communion. Venial sins on one's soul should not keep one from frequent Communion, because frequent Communion is a powerful remedy for venial sin and even takes these sins away if one is sorry for them.

There are many Catholics who, if they fall into serious sin shortly after their monthly confession and Communion, make the foolish mistake of waiting a month and longer before returning to God — just because they have gotten into the habit of not coming to the sacraments more than once a month. They place their salvation in danger rather than return quickly to God. But if a man wrecks his car, he will not wait until the next monthly inspection is due before bringing his car back to the garage to be repaired.

For the gaining of a plenary indulgence, the regular weekly confession is sufficient for all plenary indulgences to be gained during the week. For those who go to Holy Communion every day or at least five times a week, their ordinary practice of confession, whether every week or every two weeks, is sufficient for all plenary indulgences, and no special confession is required. One Communion is sufficient for all plenary indulgences of that day and the day following. All the other good works required for each plenary indulgence must be fulfilled for each indulgence to be gained.

∞

Chapter Twenty

Increase the benefits of your Communions

Sanctifying grace is increased in your soul by the very fact that you receive Communion. However, that does not mean that by receiving the sacrament you become automatically better. There are effects that depend on the cooperation and the love of the one receiving the sacrament.

Furthermore, grace does not dispense you from the moral effort, but stimulates it. What you receive in Holy Communion is not moral goodness but grace, which is a new principle of life and of goodness. That life must be lived; that principle must be used by your will. You are alive by the very fact that you have a soul, the principle of your life; but unless you actually work, you will get nothing done.

The abundance of fruit of Holy Communion is measured by the degree of your love, since the special fruit of Holy Communion is an increase of sanctifying grace and the virtue of charity. The absence of this disposition also explains why some advance so little in holiness, despite frequent Communion.

A person habitually guilty of deliberate venial sin, a person who receives Christ carelessly, thoughtlessly, without preparation and without thanksgiving, receives the benefits the sacrament produces by the very fact that he receives it, but he does not allow these benefits to grow and blossom in his heart, because he is poorly disposed. Christ does not find in these souls the willingness to permit Him to act freely in them. Their vanity, self-love, touchiness, selfishness, jealousy, and sensuality prevent the union between them and Christ from being made perfect.

After examining the various wonderful effects of Holy Communion, you will surely ask, "What is the reason these effects are not more evident in me after so many Communions?" The secret of spiritual success through Holy Communion lies in the absence of obstacles to God's grace.

When a child receives Communion, he makes no conditions. He opens his heart to God and allows God to work in him. Such an absence of obstacles is really all that is required for the sacrament to operate. The sacrament itself gives grace.

You want to be charitable, but with certain reservations: you cannot be expected to treat a certain person kindly when he has been unkind to you. You want to be pure, but you are unwilling to avoid certain circumstances that lead you into sin. You want to be patient, yet you are more anxious to have Christ take away your crosses than help you to bear them patiently. And when you keep slipping into venial sin, you try to convince yourself that you cannot be expected to be a saint and that others do worse than that.

Learn from the example of a little child to offer no resistance to the grace of God in Holy Communion so that you may benefit by its every blessing and receive its reward: the possession of God and eternal happiness in Heaven.

What matters is not so much the number as the quality of your Communions. "The more often, the better" is true, provided you receive Communion from personal conviction and not merely from routine or the desire to please. Hence, preparation and thanksgiving after Holy Communion play an important part in your spiritual life, for the fruit of Holy Communion depends on your dispositions.

Increase the benefits of your Communions

The purer the heart, the more abundant the graces of Holy Communion. Venial sin lessens the graces we would otherwise receive. To receive more abundantly the grace of Holy Communion, you should strive to be most fervent. Prepare yourself for Holy Communion by thinking of our Lord, whom you are about to receive. Make acts of faith, hope, love, and contrition.

In receiving Communion, it is not enough merely to perform an external action. There must be an interior movement of your will. For Christ to come to you, you must come to Him — that is, allow yourself to be drawn to Christ by the Father. This means yielding yourself to the action of divine grace. In seeking Jesus, you must obey the will of the Father and the inspirations of the Holy Spirit, who urges you on to divine life as a member of the Mystical Body of Christ.

Therefore, the sacrament of the Holy Eucharist, received with right and fervent dispositions, adds to your personal merits a rich bounty of grace. Approaching Holy Communion frequently, even daily, you have it in your power to become a saint. Your task is but to lay your soul open to receive this divine life, to foster it and make it grow until you become "another Christ."

∞

Communion calls for proper preparation

In receiving Holy Communion, do not be satisfied with merely performing what is necessary or obligatory. Strive so to dispose yourself as to be able to benefit by the rich graces frequent Holy Communion offers. St. Bonaventure tells us that he is persuaded that we receive more grace from one Holy Communion well prepared for than from many received with carelessness. The sacraments each contain an almost measureless treasury of grace, and, according to the perfection of your dispositions in receiving those heavenly gifts, that abundance of sacramental grace will flow into your soul.

In order that you may profit by the reception of Holy Communion, try to foster dispositions that make this union more intimate. Hence the importance of a good preparation for and thanksgiving after Holy Communion.

The following dispositions are important as a preparation for Holy Communion:

> • *Perform the duties of your state of life as perfectly as possible* in union with Jesus and in order to please Him. His whole life was a continual act of filial obedience to His Father, as He said, "I always do what is pleasing to Him."[170]
>
> Your remote preparation for Holy Communion consists in living as befits one who approaches the altar frequently, and this involves giving up whatever you feel to be a hindrance to your leading a Christian life. For example, certain pleasures and friendships that are for you occasions of sin must be sacrificed for the love of God.
>
> • *Renew your faith in the adorable Sacrament,* which is preeminently a mystery of faith. The act of faith in the Real Presence of Christ in the Sacred Host seems more wonderful than that of every other act of faith, for in this mystery, we believe not merely what we do not see, but what seems contrary to that which our senses perceive. This single act of faith will also excite you to elicit fervent acts of humility, confidence, love, and desire.
>
> • *Be sincerely humble.* This should not be difficult if you honestly consider the exalted sanctity of Jesus and your own sinfulness. Humility empties your soul of its selfishness and pride. The more you empty yourself of self, the more you will make your soul ready to let itself be possessed by God.

[170] John 8:29.

Recognizing, in the light of faith, the sovereign majesty and holiness of Him who lies concealed beneath the sacramental veils, and knowing well your own sinfulness and unworthiness, exclaim, "Lord, I am not worthy that You should enter under my roof; but only say the word and I shall be healed."[171]

To remain attached to venial sin, to deliberate imperfections, to willful negligences — all these things cannot fail to hinder Christ's action when He comes to you. Do not bargain with Christ, or reserve any place for creatures loved for their own sake. Detach yourself from creatures; aspire after perfect submission of your being to Christ by love. Christ cannot make you share in the abundance of His grace as long as you do not labor, by watchfulness over yourself and by self-sacrifice, to uproot bad habits and break off attachments to yourself and to creatures. This is true, above all, of deliberate or habitual faults against charity toward your neighbor.

• *Despite your unworthiness, turn to your sacramental God with the tenderest confidence.* Remember his kind invitation: "Come to me, all who labor and are heavy laden, and I will give you rest."[172] Draw close to Him who alone can heal your wounds, lighten your burdens, and comfort your heart.

• *Let your heart be filled with love for Jesus.* The act of love must ever hold a prominent place in your preparation for Holy Communion. The Blessed Sacrament of the Altar is a supreme manifestation of love, for in that sacrament, Jesus has poured forth all the riches of His love. Hence your heart must be aflame with love for Jesus if you wish to receive

[171] Cf. Matt. 8:8.
[172] Matt. 11:28.

those treasures of grace He has prepared for you in this heavenly banquet. Before Holy Communion, reflect on the measureless love Christ has shown you in the crib, on the Cross, and on the altar, and then exclaim with St. Thomas, "My Lord and my God!"[173] The more your heart is filled with love, the more abundantly will the graces of the Heart of Jesus pour into your soul.

• *Let your soul ardently desire the Bread of Angels.* When Jesus beholds in you a yearning desire to receive Him, He enters your soul with eager delight and lavishes upon you His choicest gifts.

He alone can give strength to your weakness and riches to your spiritual poverty. He expressed His desire of giving Himself to you when He said before the institution of the Eucharist, "I have earnestly desired to eat this Passover with you before I suffer."[174]

• *Pray.* Earnest prayer is the best preparation for Holy Communion, as it is the best thanksgiving. Ask our Lord Himself to prepare your heart, and beg our Lady to assist you in your preparation.

∞

Spend time in thanksgiving after Communion

Henry Ward Beecher said, "Gratitude is the fairest blossom that springs from the soul, and the heart of man has no flower that excels it in fragrance." Our Lord has expressed how much His Heart appreciates gratitude when He commended the grateful return of the leper whom He had cured.[175] You love those who are

---

[173] John 20:28.
[174] Luke 22:15.
[175] Luke 17:12-19.

grateful and you feel it keenly when, in return for some service you had put yourself to inconvenience to render, you meet with ingratitude. Yet ingratitude is a very common failing, and many good people do not always realize how often they fail in regard to the virtue of gratitude.

The saints realized the duty and the privilege of giving thanks. St. Philip Neri noticed that a gentleman used to leave the church almost immediately after he had received Holy Communion. He once told two altar boys to take lighted candles and to accompany the person home, one altar boy on either side. Surprised at this, the man asked the reason for their action, and the boys answered, "Father Philip told us that when the priest carries the Blessed Sacrament, he is always accompanied by two servers carrying lighted candles. The same honor is due to anyone who carries the Blessed Sacrament in his heart." Recognizing his fault, the man returned to the church and made his thanksgiving properly.

After Holy Communion, we should spend some time adoring our Lord, thanking Him, renewing our promises of love and of obedience to Him, and asking Him for blessings for ourselves and others. St. Philip Neri wanted to remind this gentleman of the presence of our Lord in his heart. It is a very common thing for Catholics to leave the church immediately after Mass, without making a further thanksgiving for the great privilege of this personal visit of Jesus in their souls. The time spent with Jesus after Holy Communion is the most precious part of the day, because Jesus is eager to grant us the graces of this sacrament, and He does so in proportion to our love and devotion.

The following dispositions are important as a thanksgiving after Holy Communion:

• *Adore Jesus* silently, conscious of your nothingness, and surrender yourself completely to Him who is your God and your all. In union with Mary, the most perfect adorer of

Jesus, bow before the majesty of God, first in the Word-Made-Flesh, and then, with Him and through Him, in the Most Blessed Trinity.

• *Speak to Jesus* reverently, confidently, and lovingly, for He is the divine Guest of your soul. Listen attentively to your Master and Friend. This is the moment in which Jesus instills in your soul His own dispositions and virtues. Lay your soul open to His divine grace.

So that your heart-to-heart talks with Jesus may not become a mere formality, vary occasionally the subject of your conversation with Him. This can be done by choosing a certain virtue, by considering some Gospel texts, or by using a favorite prayer.

You may converse with Him in any of His mysteries. Although He is now in His glorious state, you find in Him the One who has lived for you and merited for you the grace that these contain. Dwelling in you, Christ communicates this grace to you in order to bring about little by little that transformation of your life into Him which is the effect proper to this Sacrament.

You can, for example, unite yourself to Jesus as the Son of God living in the bosom of the Father, equal to His Father, God like Him, the object of His Father's good pleasure. You can speak to Him, the Incarnate Word, as our Lady did when He lived in her before being seen by the world. You can pray to Him within yourself as you would have prayed to Him, the infant Savior, two thousand years ago in the stable-cave of Bethlehem with the shepherds and Magi. He then communicates to you the grace of imitating His humility, poverty, and detachment, which you contemplate in Him in this state of His hidden life. If you desire, He will be within you the agonizing Savior, who, by His wonderful submission to His Father's will, obtains for you the grace to bear your daily crosses. He will be the divine risen Lord, who grants you the grace to detach yourself from all that is earthly, to live for God more generously and fully. He will be in you the Victor who gloriously ascends into Heaven and draws you after Him so that you may already dwell there by faith, hope, and holy desire. Christ thus contemplated and received is Christ living His mysteries over again in you. It is His life being instilled in yours with all its own beauties, merits, and graces.

Pray vocally by reciting prayers. There is no end to the inspirations of the Holy Spirit. The one thing necessary is that you recognize the greatness of the divine Gift.

• *Thank God* for the graces He has granted you, even for the dryness you may experience, which is profitable for your humility. Express your gratitude as Mary expressed her sentiments in her glorious *Magnificat*: "My soul magnifies the Lord, and my spirit rejoices in God my Savior, for He has regarded the low estate of His handmaiden. . . . He who is mighty has done great things for me, and holy is His name."[176]

• *Beg for graces* from Christ, your elder Brother, and place no bounds on your confidence. The riches of this sacrament are infinite, since it contains Christ Himself. All the fruits of the Redemption are contained in the Eucharist to become yours. Our Lord earnestly wills to give you a share in them. At Baptism, Jesus planted some tiny seeds of virtue in your soul. As the divine Sower, He comes now to see how well they are growing, to give advice and encouragement about their care, to give you will, strength, and life so that these

[176] Luke 1:46-49.

seeds of virtue may find fertile soil wherein to grow. The greater your faith and confidence, the more abundant will be the fruits your soul will receive in Holy Communion.

• *Pray for others:* for all who are dear to you, for the vast interests of the Church, for the Holy Father, bishops, and priests. Finally, conclude by asking our Lord to give you the grace of abiding in Him as He does in you, the grace of performing all your actions in union with Him in a spirit of thanksgiving. Entrust to the Blessed Virgin that same Jesus she guarded so well, in order that she may aid you in making Him grow in your heart. Thus strengthened by prayer, you may pass on to action.

The amount of time spent in thanksgiving after Communion should be about fifteen minutes. It does not seem right to hasten out of the church immediately after the priest has completed the Sacrifice, unless there is good reason for so doing.

One important way of expressing your thanks for this unspeakable gift is never to omit Holy Communion through your own fault. Another proof of gratitude is to live up to your Communion as far as you can. You must let Jesus work in your soul; and in order to do this, you have to live united to Him. The thought of your Communion received and of the one that awaits you should help you to check your natural activity so that Jesus may do His will in you. This can be done by asking yourself how Christ would have you do each action and then doing it accordingly.

∞

Participate in the Mass

The best immediate preparation for Holy Communion and thanksgiving is active participation in the Mass itself. Active participation means uniting your sentiments with those of the Victim Christ on the altar, joining the priest in offering the Holy

Sacrifice, praying with him, using, if possible, the prayers designed by the Church as they are contained in a missal or prayer book, singing parts of the Mass along with others in attendance, and serving the priest when this is necessary and permitted.

Such active participation at Mass unites you with all your fellow Christians, even to the saints in Heaven, through Christ, who offers the Sacrifice. In union with the whole Church and according to the mind of the Church, God is adored and Christ is received.

Enter into the spirit of the Mass. The drama of the Mass will take you through all the "acts" required for Holy Communion: faith, hope, love, desire, and contrition. Take your troubles, joys, and sorrows, your mistakes and failures and, uniting them with the infinite Sacrifice of Jesus, lay them on the altar in offering to the eternal Father. You have to be ready to give all to God, to accept the sufferings and trials of each day for love of Him in the same spirit that animated the Sacred Heart of Christ upon the Cross: intense love of His Father and of your neighbor, ardent desire for the salvation of souls, and full abandonment to all that He wills.

When you do this, you offer God the most acceptable homage He can receive from you, for Christ Himself takes all your sentiments into His Heart and offers perfect adoration and full satisfaction for you to His Father; He renders Him worthy thanksgiving, and His prayer is all-powerful. All these acts of the eternal High Priest by which He renews upon the altar His immolation of Calvary become yours.

At the moment of Communion, receive Jesus into your heart as the Victim who died on the Cross for your salvation. After Communion, adore, offer thanks, and make your petitions. Jesus is substantially present in the Host at least ten minutes after you receive. Remember, these moments after Holy Communion are the most precious moments of your life!

∞

Prolong your union with Christ

Even when the sacred species are consumed, you may remain closely united with Jesus. The sacred humanity is in Heaven and in the tabernacles on our altars. According to its glorious form, it is in Heaven; according to the eucharistic form, it is in the tabernacles. Assuredly, once the species are consumed, the humanity of Christ ceases to be with you according to its eucharistic state. The act itself of Communion is passing, but the effect it produces — union with Christ, the life of your soul — is meant to be permanent: it lasts as long as you wish and in the measure that you wish. Jesus does not dwell with you by His bodily presence, yet He does so by the outpourings of His love, by the lights and graces He sends you without ceasing from the tabernacle.

After Communion, grace remains. Jesus, as it were, leaves the imprint of His grace, as the soft wax retains the imprint when the seal is withdrawn. The sun is said to be in a room, not bodily, but by its rays, which produce light and warmth in the room. The tree is said to live in its branches because it constantly extends its life to them. Similarly, the God-Man never ceases to live in you, although bodily present only in Heaven and in the tabernacle; He is ever active, giving life, light, and strength to your soul by the invisible rays of His grace. He says, "Abide in me, and I in you. As the branch cannot bear fruit by itself, unless it abides in the vine, neither can you, unless you abide in me."[177] Only sin can separate you from Christ and from God. Even then the merciful Savior tries by actual graces to bring your soul back to what it has lost.

Therefore, in the course of the day, do not diminish by your carelessness, vanity, and self-seeking, the fruit of Holy Communion. It is a living Bread. The works you ought to do are the works of life, the works of a child of God, after having been nourished

[177] John 15:4.

frequently with this divine Bread in order to be transformed into Christ. Open your soul to His transforming action. Share with Him your joys and sorrows, your feelings and affections, your plans and desires. Any affection or joy you cannot share with Christ should find no room in your heart. The whole Christian life is meant to be a sharing with Christ, gradually transforming you into Christ.

A useful means of increasing and perfecting this eucharistic union is by the repetition of acts of love. If you wish to live like Jesus, you will love God as the first commandment exacts: with all your heart, with all your soul, and with all your strength.

On earth love was also the life of Jesus. He became man for the love of His Father, to reveal Him to you, and to win you for Him. Love both made Him man and nailed Him to the Cross. Love of His Father is the source of all His mysteries, of all His works and sufferings. The same love that has made Him become Bread for you retains Him in the silence of the tabernacle. In the silence of the Host, He loves His Father.

Without doubt, it is impossible for you to formulate continually definite acts of love. But you can with God's grace so multiply them that they dominate the action of your other faculties, thereby exercising on your life a more penetrating influence. It is easy to make an act of charity. A simple movement of the heart suffices. The humblest action, the least sacrifice can be transformed into an act of love. All that is done for love is love. The smallest act of pure love has more value in God's eyes than all the other acts united. Love makes you one with God. "God is love,"[178] and sanctity is union with God through love.

Another useful means of increasing and perfecting this eucharistic union is to make acts of spiritual Communion frequently during the day. Sacramental Communion is complemented by

[178] 1 John 4:8.

spiritual Communion, which makes the effects of Holy Communion even more lasting. St. Thomas Aquinas says, "He eats spiritually Jesus Christ contained in the Eucharist, if believing in Him, he desires to receive the sacrament." However, this demands the practice of recollection and generous willingness to comply with the least desire of God's holy will. Thus each spiritual Communion will be like a golden link of a chain binding one sacramental Communion to another. This certainly is a fulfillment of our Lord's last will: "Abide in me, and I in you."

The following prayer can be adopted as an act of spiritual Communion with much profit if said at definite intervals:

I believe in You, O my God,
because You are the Eternal Truth.
I hope in You, O my God,
because You are infinitely merciful, faithful, and almighty.
With my whole heart I love You, O my God,
and I am sorry for having offended You,
because You are unspeakably good and lovable.
Out of love for me, You are present in the Blessed Sacrament;
therefore I long for You, O my dearest Jesus.
Send me from the Father the Holy Spirit with His seven gifts,
that I may glorify God in all things.
Amen.

Chapter Twenty-One

Receive God's gift in Communion

For a long time, the Catholic laity of the Latin Rite did not receive Holy Communion under both species. The Church, which has authority from Christ to regulate disciplinary matters regarding the administration of the sacraments, had made that rule with a view to ensuring proper reverence toward the Holy Eucharist. Sometimes, in spite of care, there might be danger of spilling the Precious Blood of Christ.

The regulation also enabled the priest to celebrate Mass and distribute Communion without detaining the congregation for undue length of time.

This practice of Communion for the laity under one form began to spread in the thirteenth century. It serves to emphasize the Catholic doctrine that the *whole* Christ — Body and Blood, Soul and divinity — is present in *each* of the two consecrated species, under the appearances of *both* bread and wine. Therefore, there is no necessity of receiving under both species.

When Christ said, "Do this in remembrance of me," He was speaking, not to all the future members of His Church, but solely to the Apostles and their successors in the priesthood. At Mass, the priest partakes both of the consecrated Host and of the consecrated wine so that the Sacrifice may be completed.

The giving of Communion under the single form of bread is mentioned even in the days of Christ and the Apostles. Jesus said, "He who eats this Bread will live forever."[179] St. Paul wrote, "Whoever, therefore, eats the bread or drinks the cup of the Lord in an unworthy manner will be guilty of profaning the Body and Blood of the Lord."[180] In the Acts of the Apostles we read, "And they devoted themselves to the Apostles' teaching and fellowship, to the breaking of bread."[181]

∽

God gives Himself to you
through Jesus in the Mass

Mass and Holy Communion are not to be separated. It is one service, one single action, one Mass with Holy Communion as a perfect climax to the whole. This will be clearer if you consider what the Mass really is.

Mass is an offering to God. It is giving — the most beautiful and delightful of all actions.

You offer Jesus Himself, the Victim of Calvary, and thereby you present to the heavenly Father the great Sacrifice of His Son, your Brother and Savior. There is nothing greater in the world, nothing more pleasing to God, nothing more powerful.

You offer Jesus in union with the whole Church on earth. But you cannot do this without offering yourself with Him, for the Mass is the Sacrifice of the whole Christ, Head and members. The value of your offering will be proportioned to the sincerity and fervor of your self-oblation. You offer yourself with Christ and through Christ, and in that act, you unite your present offering with His offering on the Cross.

[179] John 6:58.
[180] 1 Cor. 11:27.
[181] Acts 2:42.

God gives Himself to you through Jesus at Holy Communion. Thus Mass is the meeting of God and man, of Father and children, in mutual loving self-surrender, through Christ, the only Mediator between God and men. This is the foundation of Christian holiness: union of man and God through Christ.

The very heart of the Mass is in the offering — the Consecration. Yet the Mass would be incomplete, unfinished, if it stopped there. Both its meaning and its fruit are completed by Holy Communion.

Holy Communion is the part of the Mass that most affects you, for it brings you into the Mass in a very intimate and personal way. It is not simply union with Christ; it is a sacrificial meal — that is, the eating of the Victim offered to God: Jesus, under the symbol of His sacrificial death. He said, "This is my Body given up for you. . . . This is my Blood, which is shed for you." The eucharistic Christ, before being received in Communion, has first been offered to God. The Host you receive is the Victim of the Cross, who has been offered in the Mass.

Holy Communion is the fruit of this Sacrifice. You have offered Jesus and yourself through Jesus. Communion is God's return gift. Having accepted your offering through Christ, He now gives Himself to you through Christ. At the Consecration, you have offered the heavenly Father His own beloved Son as the greatest gift you could offer Him in adoration, thanksgiving, atonement, and petition. At Communion, the heavenly Father wishes to return that gift to you as the best He can offer you. Not to receive Holy Communion would be like refusing His gift.

Therefore, the most fruitful partaking of the Sacrifice of the Altar is Holy Communion. It is also the most certain means of being transformed into Jesus, for if you are united to Christ, He immolates you with Himself, renders you pleasing to His Father, and makes you, by His grace, more and more like Himself.

∞

Chapter Twenty-Two

Overcome your misperceptions about frequent Communion

Objections that are commonly brought forward against frequent Communion are the following, and they are easily answered:

∞

"I am full of imperfections and faults"

If these imperfections and faults are the result of mere human weakness rather than of fully deliberate intention, then, instead of being obstacles, they are rather the reason you should go to Holy Communion often.

The Eucharist was instituted to deliver you from your failings and faults. It is precisely because you are weak and infirm that you take medicine. Jesus is the Physician of your soul, and His medicine is Holy Communion. Every time you go to Holy Communion, you gain strength to do right and become more pleasing to God, so that even your daily deliberate venial sins grow less numerous.

Have you not been more careful to avoid sin and to serve God well after a truly good confession and Communion? Did you not recognize how God's grace was influencing your soul? You avoided near occasions of sin, fought violent temptations, and even began to practice certain virtues and to correct certain faults. Was not all this due to the grace of Holy Communion? And if in time you grew lukewarm in God's service, voluntarily giving way to little sins, until at last you again offended God grievously, was this not the result of your neglecting Holy Communion?

It is necessary for you to receive the Holy Eucharist frequently and consistently if you are to persevere in your good resolutions. Perfection is not achieved in a day; it is the work of a lifetime.

Perhaps you feel discouraged when you remember your many faults in spite of your receiving the Holy Eucharist frequently. Those who are most keenly aware of their deficiencies are usually those who profit the most. It is a great mistake to imagine that all the effects of your Communions must be instantly visible or felt. Just as so much work has been done by the root of a plant before the tiny bud sprouts forth, so our Lord works in your soul when He visits you. He works silently, but surely, increasing your faith, strengthening your hope, deepening your charity, weaning you from the world, filling you with zeal, increasing sanctifying grace in your soul. This real progress in holiness is not incompatible with the existence of certain faults of character against which you struggle bravely but which God allows to bother you, so that you may be well grounded in humility. One excellent prayer after Communion is to ask our Lord to effect in your soul that for which He comes, for who knows as He does the special needs of your soul?

The greater your danger of losing sanctifying grace, the more urgent is your need of frequent Communion. You have to take food frequently in order to restore the bodily strength consumed in the process of life. The strength of your soul, too, is exhausted in the struggle for virtue and eternal life. You need Holy Communion to preserve the sanctifying grace you have. Christ told you that He is the food of your soul: "He who eats me will live because of me."[182] You have only yourself to blame if your soul is weak or

---

[182] John 6:57.

even dead in sins. Miss no opportunity to strengthen your soul with the graces of the Holy Eucharist. Approach the Lord's Table daily, if you can possibly do so, just because you say you are full of imperfections and faults.

∞

"I don't feel worthy to go to Communion often"

The Jansenist heretics taught that nobody is worthy to receive Holy Communion more than a few times a year. There is a strain of this heresy in this excuse. St. Pius X declared that the daily reception of Holy Communion is to be permitted to all who are in the state of grace and approach the sacrament with the intention of pleasing God and growing in virtue. He lays down no particular standard of perfection.

Do you suppose that any creature ever could be truly worthy to receive God in Holy Communion? If anyone aimed at being really worthy to receive God in this holy sacrament, he would have to equal God in sanctity. The difference between Creator and creature is so vast that the sanctity of all the saints in Heaven and on earth together would never suffice to make a soul worthy to receive Holy Communion.

If by being unworthy you mean that you are in a state of mortal sin, you can and must go to Confession, and then the obstacle will be removed. Frequent Communion will be the best means of avoiding this unworthiness in the future.

If you mean that you are full of faults, slow to do right, and careless in performing your various duties, Holy Communion is intended to be your daily Bread that acts as a remedy against your daily failings. Holy Communion is not so much a reward for virtue as it is a remedy for sin.

It is unreasonable to suppose that by waiting you will become more worthy to receive the Lord's Body. To make your unworthiness an excuse for putting off Holy Communion is as foolish as it would be to reject all food and yet desire to live. It is as senseless as it would be for a person with a high fever to say, "I will send for the doctor when I am feeling well again." If you are weak, you should go to Holy Communion more often. The more you stay away, the fewer graces will you receive, and so you will grow still weaker and still more unworthy to receive Holy Communion.

St. Ambrose writes, "Receive daily what may be daily useful. Live in such a manner that you may be worthy to receive it every day. He who is not worthy of receiving it daily, is not worthy of it even after a year."

Why can you not go to Confession at least each month? Strictly speaking, it is not necessary — although it is certainly desirable — to go to Confession, provided you have no grievous sin on your soul. If you want to be more worthy to receive, approach the Table of the Lord often.

So it would not be to the point for you to say that you do not feel worthy of receiving Jesus. No one is really worthy of this privilege at any time. You are expected to be guided not by feelings, but by the teaching of the Church.

You will not approach worthiness by abstaining from the use of the very means that most promotes sanctity. The Church knows the weakness of her children, and thus she encourages all Catholics to approach frequently the very source of the strength they need.

∞

"I can't give up my sins"

Catholics who habitually keep themselves in an unnecessary occasion of sin and thus continue repeatedly to fall into the same mortal sin may not receive Communion at all until they can bring themselves to give up both the mortal sins and their occasions.

Catholics who habitually commit a grievous sin and have no intention of giving it up fall into the same class. If they have made the final decision rather to lose their souls than to give up serious sin, they are not worthy to receive Holy Communion.

But others could break out of their terrible state of enmity with God if they would only give up the sins and their occasions and then back up that determination by a resolution to receive Communion often, even daily.

Some go to Confession and promise to give up the habit of mortal sin, but stay away from Communion for weeks and even months. They find themselves back in the old sins again. Frequent Communion is absolutely necessary if one is to break with a habit of serious sin.

∞

"I don't see any improvement in myself"

You may remain the same if you seldom go to Holy Communion, or if you receive often but without the right intention, being influenced by habit, vanity, or motives of human respect, or without the proper dispositions. However, there is no foundation at all for such a statement if you receive frequently or even daily in the state of grace, with a good intention and with sincerity. The Church would never want you to perform a religious action that is useless or even harmful.

It is true that even though you receive daily, you can and will fall into little faults. You may be irritable or excitable, obliged to associate with people with whom you are quite out of sympathy, or perhaps your selfish tendencies have remained uncorrected. Many of these imperfections are unconscious and involuntary, and may be due not to any bad habit for which you are responsible, but rather to human weakness.

Holy Communion can never directly remove all these causes of your involuntary and unconscious faults. Our Savior did not promise, nor does the Church teach, that frequent or daily Communion completely removes all voluntary sins and imperfections.

However, the Church does say that Holy Communion gives you grace to overcome your faults. Think what would become of you if you seldom went to Holy Communion! It surely is a very great grace if the frequent or daily reception of the Holy Eucharist preserves you in the state of sanctifying grace. Holy Communion affects your soul in much the same way as material food affects your body. By taking nourishment daily, a child grows in the course of time to his full stature, and the same is true of the soul: by receiving Holy Communion frequently and earnestly for years in succession, you can develop into a saint.

∞

"I feel little devotion"

Devotion that you feel is not required for a good Communion. There is a vast difference between devotion and emotion. A person can be devout without feeling it. And sensible devotion is not always the surest or most trustworthy; it is subject to many illusions.

St. Ignatius of Loyola said, "We must not abstain from the Bread of Angels because we have not sufficiently tender feelings; it would be like dying of hunger for want of honey cakes."

Holy Communion, besides increasing sanctifying grace, arouses actual love in your soul, which makes it embrace God's will joyfully and wholeheartedly. You will receive this charity if you have the right dispositions. But this love is not something that will necessarily be experienced in the feelings. For various reasons, such as fatigue, you may feel completely "dry."

The fervor produced by Communion is in the higher faculties: the mind and the will. It is conscious and deliberate adherence to God as the Supreme Good. It shows itself by devotion, which is defined by St. Thomas as the "eagerness of the will to give itself to the service of God."[183] In the midst of dryness and physical

---

[183] *Summa Theologica*, II-II, Q. 82, art. 1.

depression, your will may generously embrace the will of God: that is the heart and soul of charity.

∞

"I believe in fewer but more fervent Communions"

This is contrary to the will of Christ and the mind of the Church. It places too much stress on the importance of feeling great devotion.

Jesus gave Himself to us as food to remind us that Holy Communion is to be received frequently. The Church urges her children to accept this interpretation of Christ's words expressed in St. John's Gospel where He even warns against infrequent Communion, "Unless you eat the Flesh of the Son of Man and drink His Blood, you have no life in you."[184] The Church encourages a good preparation and thanksgiving for each Communion. The feeling of fervor that some expect is less important than the desire of Christ and the will of the Church that we receive Communion often. The Church would have us receive as often as we can and as devoutly as we can, and, when we are cold, unfeeling, and distracted, she urges us to receive anyway. Our action and our good intention are more important than our feelings.

∞

"I am afraid of losing my respect and devotion
for Holy Communion by too great familiarity"

Loss of devotion will result from improper preparation. But if you prepare devoutly for Holy Communion, frequent reception will deepen sentiments of reverence and love. Familiarity in the sense of intimacy and union with Christ is the object of all prayer and spiritual exercises. Of course, the purely mechanical reception of the sacrament with an absence of a "right and devout intention"

[184] John 6:53.

is to be avoided. This attitude is the very opposite of the one engendered by frequent Communion when care is taken to prepare properly for this great act. Virtue is a good habit. Routine indicates a facility of action that is most helpful in regard to all virtuous deeds. Hence, too, it is most desirable to make the devout reception of daily Holy Communion a matter of habitual practice, instead of being dependent upon whim or feeling.

Put aside all false ideas of reverence that keep many away from frequent Communion. Of course, the deepest possible respect is due to our dear Savior in the Sacred Host. But Holy Communion is not mainly an act of devotion, a practice of exceptional piety reserved for the few, excluding the ordinary Christian and especially children with their immature minds. With Christ and His Church, personal devotion is only of secondary importance; with them, it is a question of personal need that matters most. Because it is so necessary for the ordinary duties of everyday life, frequent — even daily — Communion is strongly recommended.

Therefore, beware of all exaggerated anxiety about going to Holy Communion, as this may only too easily prevent your approaching the Lord's Table. Go to Holy Communion in the state of grace and with a right and pious intention, thinking of Christ as your dear Redeemer, your greatest Friend and Benefactor. Make a good preparation and thanksgiving as far as your abilities and circumstances allow. Look upon Holy Communion as a remedy for all your weakness, and you will indeed receive the Holy Eucharist with the sort of reverence required by Christ and the Church.

∞

"I have no time for more frequent Communion"

People who offer this excuse are mostly those engrossed in temporal affairs. Some Catholics are so absorbed by the cares and riches and concerns of this world that they do not have time and interest enough to do something about their indifference. They don't know what they are missing. They insist on reaching out to the world for its passing pleasures and comforts, while their soul is being starved through lack of spiritual nourishment.

In the Gospel you will find a similar excuse from those who were invited to a great supper. One said, "I have bought a field, and I must go out and see it; I pray you, have me excused." Another said, "I have bought five yoke of oxen, and I go to examine them; I pray you, have me excused." Another pleaded, "I have married a wife, and therefore I cannot come." To all such the Lord replied, "I tell you, none of those men who were invited shall taste my banquet."[185]

You probably have no time because you do not wish to make time. If you have the good will, you will find time for more frequent Holy Communion. Two axioms apply here: "Where there is a will, there is a way" and "Love will find a way." The Church is far from wishing to urge you to go to Holy Communion if thereby you would be obliged to neglect the duties of your calling and position in life; but it seems that if you divide your time properly and make a conscientious use of it, you will always find that you can go to Holy Communion.

If a Catholic who says, "I'm too busy," examines his conscience, he will usually find that there is something more behind his excuse than just being too busy. Receiving Communion frequently does not require much time, perhaps half an hour. The real reason may be that he does not want to stay out of sin, or that he thinks he is good enough. He certainly lacks an informed and intelligent faith and has little personal love for Christ. If he had the proper appreciation of spiritual values, he would find time, no matter how busy his life might be.

For great numbers of Catholics, daily Communion is not an impossibility, but only a matter of sacrificing some comfort or

[185] Luke 14:18-20, 24.

convenience to keep their appointment with the Savior, who died on the Cross so that they might live. They may waste hours in idle conversations, in eating and drinking. They can find time, unhappily, for sin; they have none at all for God. What they lack is not time, but good will. Like Martha, "they are busy about many things,"[186] but they neglect the one great means — the Holy Eucharist — that will bring them the happiness they are so busy trying to attain. And yet, their main duty on earth is to serve God and save their souls. The fact that all day long they are busy about worldly affairs should be the very reason they ought to make time to go to Holy Communion. If you have once experienced the warmth and intimacy of daily union with Christ in Holy Communion, you will laugh at the trivial excuses that keep the indifferent from receiving often.

After going to Holy Communion frequently for some time, you may say, "I can't keep it up." Do as much as you can. Every Communion will help to strengthen your character, deepen your virtue, and preserve you from sin, even though you have received frequently for only a limited period.

Do not grudge the time that it takes you to go to Holy Communion, even if it costs you some trouble and sacrifice. Holy Communion is worth it. Our Savior can compensate you a thousandfold for the time devoted to Him.

∞

"I don't have time for proper preparation and thanksgiving"

There should be due preparation. But this does not mean the recitation of many prayers. The best preparation for Communion and thanksgiving is a good life and the sanctifying of your ordinary daily actions by performing them out of love for God. This can be

---

[186] Cf. Luke 10:41.

done by the use of brief, spontaneous prayers. Frequent Communion is the best preparation for Communion: one Communion is thanksgiving for another; and the Communion of today is the best preparation for the Communion of tomorrow.

St. Alphonsus says, "If you have no time to prepare yourself because of the duties of your state, do not abstain from Communion on that account. Only take care to avoid useless conversations and occupations."

If you are in the habit of going to Mass on weekdays, you can make your preparation during Mass or say the prayers of the Mass together with the priest. No preparation could be better. Spend five to ten minutes in thanksgiving after Mass if you can. This is not time wasted. You will work better and your work will be blessed after going to Holy Communion. If, however, you are able to hear Mass only on Sunday, it surely is not too much for you to devote a quarter of an hour to go to Confession at least once a month, or, if you are not in serious sin, to make an act of contrition and receive Holy Communion without Confession.

If you think about it, you will see that by staying away, you lose a twofold grace: first, that which you might have merited by ever so short a preparation and thanksgiving, and second, the sacramental grace conferred in Holy Communion. Receive Communion often, even though you have very little time at your disposal, and be sure that Christ will reward your desire for the Bread of Heaven by giving you very many graces. A pure desire to receive is enough to cause the sacrament to take effect in your soul and to preserve and increase sanctifying grace. You will be wiser if, being in the state of grace, you receive with a good intention than if you neglect to do so because you have not time to say long prayers in church before and after Communion. Yet never deliberately omit your preparation and thanksgiving or make them carelessly, because the effects of Holy Communion depend so much upon your dispositions.

∽

"I don't have time to go to Confession often"

The Church teaches that you may receive Holy Communion repeatedly without going to Confession, provided you are not conscious of any mortal sin. The *Decree on Daily Communion* explicitly states that only two conditions are required: the state of grace and a right and devout intention. Why, then, should you insert an action not required by the Church? Consequently, you may go to Communion for several weeks, if you desire, on one confession as long as you are able to keep your soul free from serious sin.

Frequent confession is recommended, because it is a sacrament and each sacrament imparts more grace, but do not let the fact that you cannot get to Confession be a reason to abstain from receiving Holy Communion, as long as you are not aware of any serious sin upon your soul. Try to confess your sins at least every two weeks.

∽

"I am a good Catholic even though I receive
the sacraments only a few times a year"

It may be that you and even your friends think you are a good Catholic because they do not receive any more frequently, but does God think so? You must judge yourself according to the standards of God and not according to the standards of men. You must save your soul the way God wants you to, and not according to the requirements people have made for themselves to suit their own convenience. If you are honest, you will have to admit that prayer and thoughts of God and eternity are not enough to keep you from sin and to make you lead a Christian life. You need other, stronger aids, and they are the sacraments — especially Holy Communion, for our Lord said, "Apart from me you can do nothing."[187] If you want to save your soul, you must keep the commandments, avoid

[187] John 15:5.

sin, receive the sacraments, and pray. The sacraments and prayer are the means of grace instituted by God. Without grace there is no salvation. Where will you get this grace if you neglect using the means, especially Holy Communion?

Some lax Catholics say, "I'm doing all right; in fact, better than a lot of people I know who receive Communion often." Such a statement indicates a lack of intelligent faith. These people think that natural goodness is sufficient, and they feel that they have no need of Christ. They fail to see that Christ made it possible for us to live a supernatural life especially through the sacrament of the Eucharist, which gives and increases that life.

To consider oneself good enough without Christ indicates pride. Usually people who do so are not doing so well even by the natural law. They build their religion not on the will of Christ, but on their own narrow standards or on the example of lax Catholics.

∞

Chapter Twenty-Three

Attain family happiness

Peace and happiness cannot exist in a family unless God lives there. Mortal sin puts God out of the home so that the Devil may preside. Satan's reign spells unrest and turmoil.

Prayer and the sacraments are sources of grace for the individual and for the family. Happiness reigns in the home insofar as these sources of grace are used, because they are the means of bringing God into the home. Special emphasis is to be placed on regular Confession and frequent Holy Communion. Confession frees you from and helps you to avoid the greatest evil in the world: sin. Holy Communion unites you most intimately with the only source of peace and happiness: God.

Nothing can be more fruitful for the preservation of love and peace in the home than frequent Holy Communion. Holy Communion is a personal visit with Jesus, the Author of all spiritual energy and of all holiness. He does not come empty-handed. He gives you an increase of sanctifying grace, which makes your soul more holy, beautiful, and pleasing to God. He gives you sacramental grace, which entitles you to special help in times of temptation and in the discharge of your duties as husband and wife toward each other and your children, or duties toward your parents as well as your brothers and sisters.

Frequent Holy Communion will enable you to obtain a complete victory over some fault or passion that may be a cause of trouble in your home. It will impart spiritual joy, sweetness, and comfort to home life in proportion to the degree to which it is possessed by the individuals who make up your family. Holy Communion wipes away venial sins and remits part, or all, of the temporal punishment due to your sins. It prepares a greater degree of eternal glory for you and all your family. Finally, no prayer for your family can be more effective than that said after Holy Communion when Jesus is present in your heart as God and man, as your best Friend, ready to help you by means of the many graces He wishes to grant you and your family, for He said, "If you abide in me . . . ask whatever you will, and it shall be done for you."[188]

If each member of your family is in the friendship of God and sanctified by the graces of Holy Communion, God really dwells in your family and there is happiness in your home. Therefore, if you are a parent, send your children to Holy Communion frequently — the more often, the better. But you must show them the way and draw them by your own good example. A good mother and father will receive Holy Communion every Sunday, if not daily. Parents and children can give no greater proof of their love for each other, nor can they do anything better to ensure happiness and God's blessing upon the family.

What an influence mothers would have on their husbands and children if they would unite themselves each morning with the Victim Jesus who offers Himself at Mass, and if they would receive Him in Holy Communion in order to obtain the many graces they need to be exemplary mothers! If you want to be transformed into a co-victim with Jesus, receive Holy Communion at Mass. It is the part of the Mass that most affects you, for it brings you into the Mass in a very intimate and personal way. Holy Communion is a

[188] John 15:7.

194

sacrificial meal — that is, the eating of the Victim offered to God. Now, if you are united with Christ, He immolates you with Himself, renders you pleasing to His Father, and makes you by His grace more and more like Himself. There is no better way of becoming a worthy father or mother, husband or wife, or child of a Christian family.

The Holy Sacrifice of the Mass is the center, the heart of our religion — a heart that, without ceasing, sends a stream of grace into the veins of Christianity, so that it may vivify each and every member of the great Mystical Body of Christ, which is our Holy Mother the Church. If the Mass is the heart of the Church, it surely is the heart of the Christian family. You could give no better proof of your love for your family than to cause each member of your family to draw closer to the Mass and to receive Holy Communion so that the Mass might draw all of you closer to the Heart of Christ and to Heaven.

Frequent Holy Communion, therefore, is the secret of happiness in the home because it brings God and His grace into the home; and where God is, there is Heaven! But most of all, through Holy Communion the family has the best guarantee of being reunited as a family in God's kingdom, for Jesus said, "He who eats my Flesh and drinks my Blood has eternal life, and I will raise him up at the last day."[189]

∞

Make the Eucharist the heart of your family

The Eucharist is the heart of the Catholic family. Christ is the source of strength for father, mother, and children. With His help, they are enabled to keep the commandments and to love God and their neighbor and one another. As a result, peace and charity reign in the family, because the eucharistic influence has

---

[189] John 6:54.

penetrated its very depths. The Christ-life, increased in their souls by frequent visits to the Table of the Lord, has become the inspiration of their every good deed. The family in which the eucharistic spirit abides is a happy family, because the peace and joy of Christ fill it. Christ reigns there supremely as in a little kingdom where He is loved, honored, and obeyed. The family in which Jesus does not live by His grace and love is devoid of His joy and blessing.

Every member of the family must do his part to bring about the reign of Christ in the home, not only by keeping the commandments and avoiding sin, but by the frequent reception of the sacraments and by prayer. The father, mother, and children should go to Holy Communion at least each month, weekly, or daily, if possible, so that they may take the eucharistic Christ into their hearts and then, as it were, bring Him home with them so that He may live there; that His spirit, which is born of love, may always abide there. Be assured, there is no better way of proving your love for your family than by bringing Christ's peace, love, and blessing into it. Neglect of regular Communion is a glaring proof that you do not have the real kind of love for your family.

If you are a father or mother, it is your duty to set a good example for your family. If the spirit of worldliness is to be kept from your home and if the truly Catholic spirit is to flourish, you must lead the way. You cannot set a better example for your family than by going to Holy Communion often. It is at once a profession of faith and the best means of maintaining the spirit of reverence, love, and obedience in your home. You little know of how much happiness you deprive your family by receiving seldom. If you are a good father and mother, you will love your children enough to make the sacrifices necessary to receive the sacraments regularly. This will mean a thousand times more for your home than your salary.

You cannot buy peace, love, or God's blessing. Those things come from God Himself, especially through Holy Communion.

What are you doing to get what is the foundation of all happiness in your family? Can you honestly say you are doing your part to bring God and Heaven into your home?

This, then, is the challenge to your generosity. Let each member — father, mother, and children — endeavor to sanctify himself by frequent contact with the eucharistic Christ, and the family will be like the Holy Family at Nazareth, with husband and wife devoted to each other in sincerest love, and children subject to their parents for the love of God. Such Eucharist-minded families are the glory of the Catholic Church.

Chapter Twenty-Four

∞

Seek the help of Our Lady of the Most Blessed Sacrament

The Blessed Virgin is called Our Lady of the Most Blessed Sacrament, because she is associated in a special way with the presence of Jesus in the Eucharist. She gave us the sacred humanity of Jesus, which is the essence of this sacrament. As St. Augustine says, "Him whom the heavens cannot contain, the womb of one woman bore. She ruled our Ruler; she carried Him in whom we are; she gave milk to our Bread."

It is to Mary, after God, that we owe the hidden "Gift of God," for Jesus is the blessed fruit of her womb. It was from her that He assumed the Flesh and Blood with which He nourishes us.

When you see Mary in Bethlehem lovingly pressing to her heart her Child, her God, it is the future eucharistic Christ. When you see Mary offering Him to the heavenly Father in the Temple for our salvation, it is the same Jesus you look upon as a Victim for our altars, whom you receive into your soul as your Guest in Holy Communion, whom you adore as your Friend in the tabernacle. He is all yours, because Mary gave her consent to become His Mother.

Although it was out of sheer goodness that God decreed to give us His own Son in the Blessed Sacrament, Mary's prayers must have had much to do with the carrying out of that plan; for she, too, must have prayed, "Give us this day our daily bread." And when Jesus instituted this holy Sacrament, He surely thought especially of His Mother.

But the relation between Mary and the Blessed Sacrament can be seen above all in her life after Good Friday, when she began her new motherhood at the feet of Jesus in the Eucharist. If to live of the Eucharist and by the Eucharist was the very special spirit of the early Church — "And they devoted themselves to . . . the breaking of bread"[190] — it must have been the summary of her last years on earth. You can easily picture St. John, the apostle of love, saying Mass each day in his own home and daily giving Mary the consecrated bread and wine of the Eucharist. There before the tabernacle, she relived in memory all the happy and sorrowful events of her life with Jesus. In her heart and life, the Eucharist took the place of His former presence in the flesh. Her ardent faith and intense love pierced the veil that separated her from her loving Son. Her heart and His burned with one flame of love to the glory of the Father there at the altar. How happy Jesus must have been to receive the homage that she paid Him! What joy He must have felt at the thought that His sacramental presence brought her such consolation!

Jesus in the Holy Eucharist is Mary's gift to you. Not satisfied with having given Himself to all mankind in the Incarnation, He wished to become united with each of us in a most intimate manner by means of the Holy Eucharist, for by an unceasing act of love, He gives Himself to us in each Consecration and in each Communion. Mary's heart is always conformable to her Son's will. Having loved her sinful children so much as to sacrifice for them her only Son in His Passion, she loved them to the end by giving them the Holy Eucharist. Every day she renews her gift generously, because

[190] Acts 2:42.

to each Sacrifice of her Son she gives her consent; each Consecration is her gift to us. Each Communion is a mystery of her love for us and a grace she obtains and bestows on us. This gift of her heart entitles her to be called Our Lady of the Most Blessed Sacrament.

∾

Our Lady is a model of eucharistic devotion

Our Lady's offering of the bloody Sacrifice of Calvary is the perfect model for your offering holy Mass. She suffered with her divine Son. Never did a mother love her son as she loved Jesus; and so never did a mother share in her son's agony so deeply as she shared in the Passion. Jesus died because He willed to die. Mary must have willed her Son's death, because, hard as it was to make this sacrifice, it would have been quite impossible for her will to be the least separated from His. He died out of love for us; this was His final proof of love. Aside from the Sacred Heart of Jesus, no human heart ever loved mankind so deeply as Mary's heart, and therefore she wanted to unite her will to His, offering to Almighty God this Holy Sacrifice out of pure charity for the human race.

Mary is truly your model in offering holy Mass. Ask Our Lady of the Most Blessed Sacrament to help you share actively in holy Mass by sharing in her spirit. She will teach you to imitate her by accepting willingly all the suffering that your service of God involves, your struggles against temptation, your difficult acts of virtue, your little penances — in union with the Victim Jesus on the altar, out of love for God and mankind.

Our Lady of the Most Blessed Sacrament earnestly invites you to come and partake of this Bread of Life. It is through her that you are able to eat the Bread of Heaven even every day. It is through her prayers that God inspires you to receive it and grants you the grace to receive it frequently. Each time Jesus becomes present in the hands of the priest, the Life given to us by the words of consecration comes originally from Mary. Surely it is through her special influence as Mediatrix of Graces that this Life is shared with you. Therefore, offer Jesus to the Father through her hands, and in Holy Communion ask for graces through her.

From her early years, Mary adored the one true God in the Temple at Jerusalem. She adored her God incarnate within her chaste womb from the time of the Incarnation to His birth. In Bethlehem she first adored Him in His visible presence as He lay in all His helplessness before her joyful eyes. From that time forward until His Ascension into Heaven, she was the constant adorer of the Word-Made-Flesh in all the mysteries of His earthly life. The early Christians, all lovers of the Eucharist, who visited her frequently during her hidden life of adoration, must have taken away with them the spirit of her eucharistic devotion. As she knelt before the Sacred Species, she truly influenced them to be ardent lovers of her loving Son in the Blessed Sacrament.

Ask Our Lady of the Most Blessed Sacrament to teach you to prove your love for Jesus by visiting Him frequently in His tabernacle home, where He lives as the best Friend you have upon earth, ready to console and strengthen you in your trials.

It is the eucharistic work of Mary to draw souls to Jesus in the Blessed Sacrament. Since the Eucharist is the source from which the graces of Redemption continually flow to mankind, what an ardent longing must burn in the heart of the Blessed Virgin Mary for the flourishing of devotion to the Blessed Sacrament! How earnestly she must stand at the side of the priest at the altar, encouraging him with devotion; how her loving hand guides her children to receive Communion! The more the love and veneration of Mary is fostered, the more does devotion to the Eucharist flourish.

Through Mary we receive every grace and, consequently, those graces contained in the Most Holy Sacrament of the Altar. The graces which come to us through the intercession of our Lady are such as to move men toward the fruitful reception of the Blessed

Eucharist. Dwelling now and forever in the glory of Heaven, she draws those for whom Christ died on the Cross to the Eucharist and disposes them to live even more perfectly with the eucharistic life. She was the first to practice the duties of a truly eucharistic life, showing us by her example how we ought to assist at Mass, receive Holy Communion, and visit the Most Blessed Sacrament.

Choose Mary as your model of eucharistic devotion. Offer holy Mass, receive Holy Communion, and visit Jesus in the tabernacle in union with her, in the spirit in which she herself did so. Just as in your tenderest years you learned to love God at your mother's knee, so now learn to love your eucharistic God, as it were, at her knee, for you can safely believe that Mary is the shortest and surest way to the Heart of the eucharistic Christ.

May our Lady lead you to your sacramental Jesus! May she make you a fervent apostle of the Eucharist! May she make you Eucharist-minded to the extent that your very life may be the Eucharist — in union with her, Our Lady of the Most Blessed Sacrament.

Chapter Twenty-Five

Offer praise and thanksgiving for the Eucharist

We could never put into words the marvels that God's love has gathered up in the Eucharist. He needed no creature to increase His glory. He would have been perfectly happy without your love, and yet in divine compassion He revealed to you the wonders of His glory as God and man and the tenderness of His love in the Sacrament of the Altar. He stooped to you to share with you the treasures of His divinity, leaving with you a foretaste of Heaven.

The Eucharist is the jewel of all God's gifts to mankind, for in it you can enjoy His overflowing kindness. It contains all His perfections, and there is nothing that your heart can rightly desire that cannot be found in it. His eternal wisdom could not have devised a union more intimate. His divine power could not have prepared for your soul a food more delightful or a treasure more precious. His infinite goodness could not have been poured out upon your soul more abundantly than through this Sacrament, in which are enclosed all His divine riches, all under the lowly form of an earthly gift of bread and wine. Truly, the Eucharist is a summary of the marvels of His love toward you. This Mystery of Love came forth from His very Heart.

The Basic Book of the Eucharist

What would our Christian religion be without the Eucharist? If the Blessed Sacrament were taken away, the Church would be no more. She has everything because Jesus is with her. All her riches, all her light, all her strength, grace, and beauty come to her from Him. He is the foundation of her unity, her activity, and her very existence. The Holy Eucharist — the Real Presence, holy Mass, Holy Communion — is the Church's first and most sublime object of devotion and love, her treasure. The Holy Eucharist is the center of the Catholic religion, the very heart of our Faith, and the source of our happiness.

Eternal praise and thanks to You,
Jesus Christ,
Son of God made man,
born of the Blessed Virgin,
for the mercy and love You have shown
to Holy Mother Church,
and to me in particular,
in this sacrament.

I unite my voice of praise
and my sentiments of love
with those of the angels and saints in Heaven,
with Mary — their Queen, and
Our Lady of the Most Blessed Sacrament —
and with all Your faithful children on earth.

I thank You,
divine Word Incarnate,
for the Real Presence
of Your Body and Blood,
Soul, and divinity
among us under the veils of bread and wine;
for Your Sacrifice of Calvary,

Offer praise and thanksgiving for the Eucharist

renewed in an unbloody manner
on our altars at holy Mass,
at which we offer You to God
as a Victim worthy of His Majesty and
as a Gift that fulfills all our obligations to Him;
for the supreme privilege
of receiving You as the Bread of Life
and of being united so closely to You
in Holy Communion.

May my whole life be an unending hymn
of praise and thanksgiving to You
for this most wonderful Gift: the Eucharist!

O Sacrament most holy,
O Sacrament divine,
All praise and all thanksgiving
Be every moment Thine!

Lawrence G. Lovasik

Lawrence G. Lovasik
(1913-1986)

"Life is short, and we must all give account of it on the Day of Judgment," said Fr. Lawrence Lovasik. "I am in earnest about using the time allotted to me by God on this earth to the best advantage in carrying out the ideal of my life — to make God more known and loved through my writings."[191]

The oldest of eight children, Lawrence Lovasik was born of Slovak parents in the steel-industry town of Tarentum, Pennsylvania. He was accepted into the Sacred Heart Mission Seminary in Girard, Pennsylvania, at the age of twelve and, after thirteen years of study and training, was ordained to the priesthood at St. Mary's Mission Seminary in Techny, Illinois, in 1938. Fr. Lovasik studied further at Rome's Gregorian Papal University, spent three years as a teacher and prefect of seminarians, and went on to do missionary work in America's coal and steel regions. In 1955, he founded the Sisters of the Divine Spirit, an American religious congregation of home and foreign missionaries whose services included teaching, visiting homes, and assisting in social work.

[191] Walter Romig, *The Book of Catholic Authors*, 5th ser. (Grosse Pointe, Michigan: Walter Romig and Company, 1943), 181.

Fr. Lovasik devoted much of his time to giving missions and retreats. These experiences and that of his earlier missionary work acquainted him with the spiritual needs, personal and family problems, and individual plans and longings of God's people, and he yearned to help them. Christ's exhortation to His first priests — "Go, and make disciples of all nations"[192] — was his inspiration. "I wanted to reach the hearts of people," he said, "but my voice could be heard only by those to whom I was able to preach."[193] Writing, he found, was his way to preach God's love and truth to the many, and it was his personal love for Christ, for the Blessed Mother, and for all immortal souls that drove him to dedicate as much time as possible to this talent.

Prayer and the Holy Eucharist are the emphases of many of the several books and more than fifty pamphlets that Fr. Lovasik wrote. His style is simple, sincere, and highly practical. He combines his vision of the transforming power of holiness and his compassionate understanding of man's desires and weaknesses to offer sound spiritual direction that motivates and inspires his readers, leads them step by step toward holiness, warns them against spiritual and temporal pitfalls, and guides them back to the right path when they go astray. Fr. Lovasik's wisdom not only reveals the often overlooked strength of holiness, but also continues to make real his life's ideal — to make God more known and loved.

---

[192] Matt. 28:19.
[193] Romig, *The Book of Catholic Authors*, 180.

Sophia Institute

Sophia Institute is a nonprofit institution that seeks to nurture the spiritual, moral, and cultural life of souls and to spread the Gospel of Christ in conformity with the authentic teachings of the Roman Catholic Church.

Sophia Institute Press fulfills this mission by offering translations, reprints, and new publications that afford readers a rich source of the enduring wisdom of mankind.

Sophia Institute also operates two popular online Catholic resources: CrisisMagazine.com and CatholicExchange.com.

Crisis Magazine provides insightful cultural analysis that arms readers with the arguments necessary for navigating the ideological and theological minefields of the day. *Catholic Exchange* provides world news from a Catholic perspective as well as daily devotionals and articles that will help you to grow in holiness and live a life consistent with the teachings of the Church.

In 2013, Sophia Institute launched Sophia Institute for Teachers to renew and rebuild Catholic culture through service to Catholic education. With the goal of nurturing the spiritual, moral, and cultural life of souls, and an abiding respect for the role and work of teachers, we strive to provide materials and programs that are at once enlightening to the mind and ennobling to the heart; faithful and complete, as well as useful and practical.

Sophia Institute gratefully recognizes the Solidarity Association for preserving and encouraging the growth of our apostolate over the course of many years. Without their generous and timely support, this book would not be in your hands.

www.SophiaInstitute.com
www.CatholicExchange.com
www.CrisisMagazine.com
www.SophiaInstituteforTeachers.org